W9-BKI-140

DATE DUE

WITHDRAWN

Break Down Your Money

Break Down Your Money

HOW TO GET BEYOND THE NOISE TO PROFIT IN THE MARKETS

Tracy Byrnes

WILEY

John Wiley & Sons, Inc.

Published by John Wiley & Sons, Inc., Hoboken, New Jersey.
Published simultaneously in Canada.

For general information on our other products and services or for technical support, please contact our Customer Care Department within the United States at (800) 762–2974, outside the United States at (317) 572–3993 or fax (317) 572–4002.

Wiley also publishes its books in a variety of electronic formats. Some content that appears in print may not be available in electronic books. For more information about Wiley products, visit our web site at www.wiley.com.

Library of Congress Cataloging-in-Publication Data:

Byrnes, Tracy
    Break down your money : how to get beyond the noise to profit in the markets / Tracy Byrnes.
      p. cm.
    Includes bibliographical references and index.
    ISBN 978-0-470-22680-3 (cloth)
      1. Stocks. 2. Bonds. 3. Portfolio management. 4. Investments.
      5. Saving and investment I. Title. II. Title: Profit in the markets.
  HG4661.B97 2008
  332.63–dc22

                                          2008002737

  ISBN-13 978–0–470–22680–3

Printed in the United States of America
10 9 8 7 6 5 4 3 2 1

To my angels,
David, Julia, and Celia,
I love you more than peanut butter.

Contents

Foreword

In a perfect world, investing in the stock market would be a fair competition, like running onto a level playing field to engage in a game of football where neither team has the opening advantage. But investing, you may have already learned, is anything but fair.

Unless you're one of the savvy Wall Street insiders, joining the investment game can be like getting thrown onto the field with a couple of cracked ribs, bruised knees, no shoulder pads . . . and no team behind you.

Enter Tracy Byrnes. With this book, Tracy has done something few writers have been successful at accomplishing: helping the rest of us understand, maneuver around, enter into, and profit from the smashmouth game known as successful investing.

Since 1930, the stock market has returned an average of 11 percent per year. On a good day, your basic bank account or money market will cough up, at best, 4 to 5 percent. So as scary as it might be with all its confusing terminology and often frightful news swirling around on a daily basis, the stock market will, over the long term, get you the most bang for your buck. Tracy, an accomplished certified public accountant and shrewd financial journalist, has picked apart the insider's playbook and has turned it inside out, translating the lexicon and explaining the way things *really* work so that you can get to work putting your money in the game.

No other book about the markets provides the kind of sweeping insights, comprehensive explanations, and analogies that Tracy has formulated.

Whether we're facing a consumer or banking credit crunch, mortgage woes, a dot-com implosion, a real-estate crisis, a savings and loan disaster, or something akin to the Tulip Mania of the 1600s, every decade may bring uncertainty, risk, and loss. That is what makes Tracy's book so valuable, not just to the novice investor, but even to the experienced few who think they've already made it to the Super Bowl of investing. History has proven that even the savviest investor can get sucked into beguiling market games, only to get beaten badly on the field.

We all deserve a fair shot at saving for our future, for our retirement, for our children's college education, for our hopes and dreams. By turning the pages of this book, you've already scored a touchdown. Get ready for that level playing field, with Tracy Byrnes as your winning quarterback.

LIZ CLAMAN
New York, NY
April 2008

Introduction

So, have you checked the stock market today?

Stop laughing.

I know. In between 10-hour workdays, your kid's soccer games, and your constantly sabotaged attempts to get to the gym, who has the time to care about whether Microsoft's earnings release moved the stock price up or down?

Who even knows what that means? What exactly is an "earnings release" and why is it moving the stock? Market pros have created their own professional lingo, and if you're not in the know, it's just gibberish. But it's important gibberish that can make you some serious money, so it's high time you learned the language.

That's where this book comes in.

The stock market is the cornerstone of everything we do. Whether you're an artist, a dentist, or a stay-at-home mom, you need to understand how the economy and the stock market play together. Odds are good you're saving for a house, retirement, or your next vacation; so why not learn how to make that money work for you? The S&P 500 is up about over 26 percent over the last five years. This means that if you invested $10,000 in the market on January 1, 2002, you would have earned an extra $2,600 by the end of 2007!

Movements in the market also determine how much money comes into your home on a daily basis. When stocks are doing well, that usually means the underlying companies are doing well. That could equate to new job opportunities or raises for people who work for those companies. That's all good news for your household.

I'm not asking you to start spending your free time investing. Who has free time? Nor do I expect you to quit your job and start trading stocks for a living. This book is here so that when you turn on the TV in the morning, you'll know what it means when the talking heads report that the S&P futures were down overnight, or that the market might start the day off a bit shaky. If you glance at a newspaper headline and it says that Coca-Cola increased its quarterly dividend, you will know that means the company has some extra cash on hand and has decided to give it back to the shareholders. If you happened to find a little time and have the inclination to dive in and play, you'll then be armed with enough knowledge to compete with the professionals.

This book is broken down into three parts. The first covers the basics: an overview of the market, definitions of stocks, bonds, mutual funds, and so on. The second part dives into the financial statements and provides an understanding of the Federal Reserve and how it influences the markets. The final part gives you some great metrics to help you understand how your favorite stocks are doing compared to their peers. This is also where we pull it all together and help you establish a game plan so that you can create a sound investment portfolio.

We're covering a lot of ground, but the chapters are short because you and I don't have the time or attention span for long-winded anything. The chapters and different topic sections are short enough to read during coffee breaks, bathroom breaks, time-outs, or on the sidelines of your kid's soccer game. So keep it with you, pick it up when you can, and start to get smart about the market.

And did I mention we'll be talking about cars, James Bond, and beer, too? I told you—we're going to have fun.

Acknowledgments

Never in a million years did I think I'd write a book. If it weren't for the people listed below, I probably would've never done it. With that, I send my heart and my thanks to:

Tricia Davey, my agent, for believing in me enough to peddle my book proposal all over town.

Laura Walsh, editorial program coordinator at John Wiley & Sons, for actually buying it.

Emilie Herman, my editor, for keeping me and my book focused and calm.

Dan Colarusso for being my Dalai Lama.

My girlfriends for, well, you know.

My "strategic advisor," Pierre Swart, for, well, you know, too.

My children, David, Julia, and Celia, for inspiring me to do fabulous things for them. I just hope they're proud of me someday.

My brother, Paul, for being my ever-faithful rock and best friend.

My stepfather, Jim, for wholeheartedly taking on the role of father and grandfather.

And most importantly, my mother. I'm sorry it took me 35 years to get it. You will never know how much I admire you and how hard I have tried to emulate you throughout the years. Your constant encouragement and choruses of *Climb Every Mountain* are the reason I am who I am today. *Ti amo.*

Finally, I send my heart and my thanks to God, for blessing me with all of the above the people.

BE AN OWNER, NOT AN EMPLOYEE

CHAPTER 1

To Market to Market, to Buy a . . . What?

These days the stock market is everywhere. From newspaper headlines to cocktail conversation, it's as ubiquitous as Paris Hilton. And it's talked about just like Paris. "Paris Wants a New TV Show." "The Market Wants the Fed to Cut Rates."

Who or what is this "market" and how dare he (or she?) make such demands?

Let's clear things up. This omnipresent "market" is not human. (It does act like my three-year-old at times, but we'll get to that in a bit.) Nor is it a place where you can buy blueberries or sweet corn in the middle of your town square on a beautiful Saturday afternoon. However, there *will* be a bunch of buyers and sellers at this market and you will need money if you plan on taking something home. But you're not taking home fresh produce or a handmade wicker basket. Instead, you're going to buy and sell stocks, bonds, options, and exchange-traded funds.

Way more fun than a wicker basket.

So What Exactly *Is* the Stock Market?

The *stock market* refers to a place where you can buy or sell stocks. There are three big stock exchanges in the United States:

- *The New York Stock Exchange (NYSE).* The NYSE is the oldest and most popular organized stock exchange in the United States. It is kind of like the Bergdorf Goodman of stock exchanges. Most of the big-time companies such as General Motors, Johnson & Johnson, and Nordstrom (naturally) are all here on the NYSE.
- *The American Stock Exchange.* You might know this exchange as the *Amex.* It is smaller than the NYSE and the companies that you can trade there also tend to be smaller and sometimes more risky than those listed on the NYSE. You can buy exchange-traded funds here, which are fabulous, and we'll delve into those later in the book.
- *The Nasdaq.* The name of this exchange (pronounced naz-dack) stands for the National Association of Securities Dealers. Technology stocks have found a home here. So, at the Nasdaq, you'll find Microsoft, Google, and Yahoo!.

Companies that are traded on these exchanges are abbreviated with a special *ticker symbol,* an abbreviation that may not always clue you in on what stock is meant. For example, Microsoft, which is traded on the Nasdaq, is MSFT. Its competitor, Apple, is AAPL, which is also traded on the Nasdaq. These symbols can be used, as well as the company names, to get stock quotes and other information at various online resources. We will learn more about ticker symbols—and online resources—later in this chapter and throughout this book.

There are also additional smaller exchanges in other major U.S. cities such as Chicago and San Francisco. But most of the action happens on the three listed above.

Overseas, London and Tokyo are some of the big cities that also have major stock exchanges, which are important no matter where you call home. Just like we take our fashion cues from the catwalks of Paris, what happens in London and Tokyo overnight helps us gauge our markets when we wake up. We'll tackle how those markets affect us later in the book.

But here's the catch: You can't actually go to these markets.

What? Can't go to the store? Can't wander the aisles? Sample the perfume? Test drive the car?

Nope.

The NYSE and the Amex do have actual buildings down in the Financial District of New York City, though the Amex will probably move in with the NYSE, since the NYSE agreed to acquire the Amex in January 2008. Rent the movie *Wall Street* with Michael Douglas, who played the infamous Gordon Gekko, and you'll get an idea of what the district looks like. (Parts of the movie were actually filmed on Wall Street. Others look like they were shot in Utah, but you'll get the idea.) But again, you can't go shopping there.

And the Nasdaq is totally electronic. While there is an actual building with corporate offices, it's basically a fake storefront, strictly for the tourists.

A (Very) Brief Walk Down Wall Street

Wall Street—named for a real wall built by Dutch colonists in 1653—has been a financial hub since 1792, when 24 men signed an agreement to start the New York Stock Exchange (NYSE) at 40 Wall Street (which is now a Trump building, no surprise).

For a long time Wall Street was just a dirt path leading to the East River, where merchants traded paper shares of a ship's cargo on the piers so they wouldn't have to carry large amounts of gold or silver. The Bank of New York was the first company that traded on the NYSE in 1792.

In the 1920s, the NYSE outgrew its space and moved to 11 Wall Street, where it's still located today.

Source: NYSE Euronext.

Think of the stock market as your favorite department store. My favorite is Nordstrom. The biggest reason I go to Nordstrom is its fabulous shoe department. The icing on the cake is that I can get a lipstick and a trendy new blouse to go with my new fabulous shoes without ever leaving the store.

So consider the NYSE as a department store of stocks. Actually it's more like a flea market because buyers and sellers can peddle their goods. Department stores, however, have much cleaner bathrooms, so we'll stick with that analogy for now. Just remember, you can't visit this department store; but traders can—the ones who have a seat.

NYSE: The Best Seat in the House

We've all paid top dollar for a good seat. I once paid $1,000 to get a front-row seat to a Bruce Springsteen concert. (Don't tell anyone!) But to get one of the 1,400 seats at the NYSE, you'll need to pony up anywhere from $500,000 to $1,000,000 apiece. The big brokerage houses such as Goldman Sachs and Morgan Stanley own as many as 20 seats at a time.

I've never been clear on why there are actual seats, since no one is ever *in* them. All of the trading happens down on the trading floor. If you turn on the FOX Business Channel and see a bunch of crazy people in colorful jackets, those are the traders who are supposed to be in those million-dollar seats. And to think, I have the nerve to get mad at my daughter when she doesn't stay in her seat at a $15 show.

Quick fashion factoid: The exchange requires floor traders to wear jackets (me too when I report from down there). In the old days, when traders where literally running from one end of the floor to another to get a trade in on time, the exchange realized that wearing a suit was too constricting and designed more comfortable trading jackets. They look like short versions of a doctor's lab coat. The firms are color-coordinated so that their people can easily spot each other on the floor. Certain firm members wear blue coats while others wear green or pink, which is my personal favorite.

Investors and the public are not allowed to be on the floor. The closest you can come to that exchange trading floor is by watching financial networks such as FOX Business Network— you are watching, right? If you want to buy a share of one of the 3,600 companies listed on the NYSE, you'll have to call your broker or log onto your online brokerage account to do that. Your broker will relay your trade request to those folks in the colorful trading jackets on the floor and they'll make the trade on your behalf. That's why you'll have to pay your broker a commission—anywhere from $10 to $100 per trade—for providing this service to you.

The Amex works the same way. It only lists around 1,000 stocks and offers about 660 seats for its traders.

Nasdaq: Online Dating Service

The Nasdaq works differently. Think of the Nasdaq as a telecommunications network. There are no people running around. Instead, technology matches buyers with their appropriate sellers. You call your broker and tell her you want to buy some shares of Apple, which lists on the Nasdaq with abbreviation AAPL. She can't get in touch with the people on the trading floor because there is no trading floor. Remember, the Nasdaq is just a storefront building. Instead, she contacts a dealer who puts your order into the system and, *voila!,* Your match is made.

You now know how the markets work. With the help of your broker, you can buy stocks (as well as bonds and exchange-traded funds, which we'll get to in a bit). And buying stocks can make you money.

So the next logical question is: What should I buy?

Buy a Stock and Become a Restaurateur

When you buy a stock, you're basically buying a small piece of the company that you chose to invest in. That means you own a fractional piece of everything—the buildings, inventories, computers, and so on. Of course, you also own an equivalent piece of the company's debts and IOUs.

A stock used to be an actual certificate, like the one your kid gets in school for completing the 50-yard dash. A *stock certificate* was basically your prize for buying a share of the company. Some of you may still have some left over from the old days. Nowadays you don't get that congratulatory piece of paper. Odds are good you'll just get an e-mail confirmation stating the trade was made. Print that out and save it with your trading documents for future reference.

So how do you become a stockholder? Before we can answer that question, you have to be willing to invest in a company.

Let's say your buddy just opened this great sushi joint in town and you want a piece of it. The restaurant is worth $1 million, and he offers you 10 percent. You pony up $100,000 and you're now a 10 percent shareholder, another way of saying a stockholder, in the hottest restaurant in town. As a shareholder, you now have a vested interest in the business so you clearly want your sushi restaurant—your company—to make money. That means your friend better sell a boatload of sushi. And let's presume he does. If he ends the year with a net profit of $500,000, then 10 percent, that is, $50,000, goes in your pocket. See, ownership does have its privileges.

But your friend's restaurant is a *privately held company*. Basically he's keeping his investors amongst himself—he's keeping things private. A privately held company does not have a stock that's listed on an exchange.

A stock that is listed on an exchange is called a *publicly held company*, which means anyone from the public can buy in. But the same philosophy applies. If you buy YUM! Brands shares, you will own a piece of KFC, Pizza Hut, Taco Bell, Long John Silver's, and A&W All-American Food Restaurants. (I just love a good root beer float.) Again, you're a restaurateur, only this time in a public company with a much smaller piece of ownership.

As a shareholder, you're rooting for KFC to sell tons of chicken, Pizza Hut to score on those cheese sticks, and you're really hoping that the root beer float makes a comeback. The more product YUM! sells, the more money the company makes. As a shareholder, that means you make money, too.

Rock the Vote

Another perk to being a shareholder is that you get to vote on some company decisions. Obviously, the more shares you own, the more voting power you have.

Granted, you don't get to vote on whether the office bathroom should be painted cream or baby blue. Nor do you get to vote on new products that come down the pipeline. You *do* get to vote on bigger issues such as whether the company should issue more stock or who should be on the board of directors. (That's a very important vote, by the way.)

Companies have shareholder meetings when a vote is needed and you can attend and vote in person. When Warren Buffett schedules shareholder meetings for his holding company Berkshire Hathaway in Omaha, Nebraska, shareholders come out in droves. A whopping 27,000 people showed up at the 2007 meeting. Known as "Woodstock for Capitalists," there are cocktail receptions, barbeques, and dinners. Not to mention, many of the companies that Berkshire holds are there to represent their products. So you can buy insurance from Geico and get an ice cream cone from Dairy Queen. In addition, the Q&A sessions are actually informative and interactive.

That is *so* not the norm! Most shareholder meetings are boring and uninspiring, and you certainly don't get free ice cream. That's why many shareholders vote via proxy ballot. A proxy ballot is a substitute for your absence at the corporate meeting. Basically you get your ballot at home, vote, and drop it in the mail by the required date.

Whether you road trip to a stockholder's meeting or mail in the proxy, you should vote. Every vote counts—as Al Gore can tell you. (In 2000, Bush won Florida by a measly 327 votes, in case you forgot.)

Skip First Class

There are two types of stock: common and preferred.

Common stock is what we've been talking about—a piece of ownership in a company. *Preferred stock* also represents a piece of ownership. Preferred stock shareholders, however, don't have any voting rights, nor do they get to enjoy the stock's upside. Preferred shareholders are paid a fixed dividend that does not fluctuate.

The big benefit to owning preferred stock is that preferred shareholders get paid first when the company is dishing out its profits. Common shareholders are paid afterwards, but common shareholders are paid based on the stock's price. So if the price goes up, the common shareholders get paid more. The preferred folks still get their same old dividend, which isn't a bad thing when the stock falls and the common stockholders are losing their shirts. So they're less of a gamble. Still, in most instances, you're better off with the common shares and that's what we'll refer to for the rest of the book.

So Where's My Money, Honey?

So you now own a piece of a company, but you don't have anything tangible. How do you cash in on your profits?

Let's say you buy YUM! at $32 and Pizza Hut comes out with a fat-free pizza that sells like mad. The stock soars to $50. You just made $18. But you don't really have the money in your pocket, do you? Nope. The pros call that a *paper gain* because you only see that gain when you log on to your brokerage account and jump up and down because the stock price went up.

To get that $18 into your hands, you need to call your broker and tell him you want to sell the *actual share*. Then he'll send you $50, less some small processing fee. Remember, you spent $32 to get that $50, so you're total gain is only $18. But that's not bad considering all you did was sit back and watch people stuff their faces with pizza. You'll also owe Uncle Sam taxes on that gain. Nevertheless, the end result is that you've made money, but you lost ownership.

If you believe the folks at KFC will soon come out with a fat-free version of the Colonel's chicken, then you might want to hold on to that stock a little longer in hopes that it goes up. It sounds like a gamble, but later on in this book you'll learn how to make some smart buy/sell decisions. For now, just relish in the fact that people are eating and you're making money!

Look to the Indexes for the Market Scoop

You now know the privileges of ownership, and why you should own stocks—either outright or through a mutual fund, which we get to in Chapter 4. How do you figure out what to buy and when? With 10,000 stocks available to trade, there's no way to go through all of them and see which stocks are trading higher or lower at a particular point in time. So you need to read something that can give you an overall sense of what the market is doing.

When you want to know what's going on in the sports world, you tune in to ESPN. When you want to know what's up—or down—in the stock market, you need to check the major market indexes and averages. Market indexes were created to give people the general gist of how stocks are doing, a sort of cheat sheet, if you will.

A stock market index is a sampling of stocks used to measure market performance. The stocks that make up these indexes are selected based on some commonality—like trading on the same stock market exchange or belonging to the same industry. Each index offers a snapshot of what the market is doing. So, just like ESPN gets you into the locker room of your favorite team, the major stock market indexes get you the inside scoop on the market.

Inside the Locker Room

For broad market information, investors, traders, and TV pundits use the Dow Jones Industrial Average, the Standard & Poor's 500 Index, and the Nasdaq Composite. These three indexes give you a great idea of what the market is doing, so it's important you get to know them and what they represent.

The Dow The Dow Jones Industrial Average (DJIA, or just "the Dow") is published by the *Wall Street Journal,* believe it or not. The editors actually select the stocks that are included in the average. It seems odd that such an important index is determined by a bunch of journalists. (I'm a journalist. I get to say that!)

The Dow was first published in 1896 and tracked only 12 stocks. In 1928, near the height of the Roaring Twenties, 18 more stocks were added and the list has stayed at 30 stocks that trade on the NYSE ever since.

Calculating the value of the Dow began as a fairly simple computation. Stock prices were added up and that number was divided by the number of stocks in the average. Things got more complicated as companies merged and stocks split and others are added and removed.

These days, many argue that the Dow doesn't really paint an accurate picture of the overall stock market because the equation places more value on high-priced stocks than low-priced ones. That's because a big change in just one high-priced stock could cause the average to give a false reading of the market. The Dow might also be too small to represent the entire market because it follows only 30 of roughly 3,000 stocks traded on the NYSE. Since it doesn't track many consumer goods or technology stocks (because many of those are on the Nasdaq), it's missing some of the companies that play a huge role in our economy—such as Microsoft, Apple, and Research in Motion (RIMM), which gave us the handy and ubiquitous BlackBerry.

Still, you can't turn the TV on or click to your favorite financial web site without hearing about the value of the Dow, which was around 12,600 in early April 2008. The 30 companies that make up the Dow these days are listed in Table 1.1, as are their ticker symbols.

The S&P 500   Created by the Standard & Poor's Corporation in 1923, the S&P 500 is composed of 500 U.S. stocks from both the NYSE and the Nasdaq. It's a much broader index than the Dow because it follows more sectors, including financials, information technology, and health care. After the Dow, the S&P 500 is the most widely watched index of U.S. stocks.

A big difference between the Dow and the S&P 500 is how their values are calculated. While the Dow looks only at stock prices, the S&P 500 looks at the total "market value" of each stock in the index. A stock's total market value is found by multiplying its share price by the number of outstanding shares. If the stock of Company A is trading at $30 and there are 100,000 shares out there, the company's market cap is $3 million.

Table 1.1   The Dow Jones Industrial Average List of Companies

Company	Exchange and Ticker Symbol	Industry
3M	(NYSE: MMM)	Diversified industrials
Alcoa	(NYSE: AA)	Aluminum
American Express	(NYSE: AXP)	Consumer finance
American International Group	(NYSE: AIG)	Full-line insurance
AT&T	(NYSE: T)	Telecoms
Bank of America	(NYSE: BAC)	Banks
Boeing	(NYSE: BA)	Aerospace/defense
Caterpillar	(NYSE: CAT)	Commercial vehicles & trucks
Chevron	(NYSE: CVX)	Integrated oil & gas
Citigroup	(NYSE: C)	Banks
Coca-Cola	(NYSE: KO)	Beverages
DuPont	(NYSE: DD)	Commodity chemicals
ExxonMobil	(NYSE: XOM)	Integrated oil & gas
General Electric	(NYSE: GE)	Diversified industrials
General Motors	(NYSE: GM)	Automobiles
Hewlett-Packard	(NYSE: HPQ)	Diversified computer systems
Home Depot	(NYSE: HD)	Home improvement retailers
Intel	(Nasdaq: INTC)	Semiconductors
IBM	(NYSE: IBM)	Computer services
Johnson & Johnson	(NYSE: JNJ)	Pharmaceuticals
JPMorgan Chase	(NYSE: JPM)	Banks
McDonald's	(NYSE: MCD)	Restaurants & bars
Merck	(NYSE: MRK)	Pharmaceuticals
Microsoft	(Nasdaq: MSFT)	Software
Pfizer	(NYSE: PFE)	Pharmaceuticals
Procter & Gamble	(NYSE: PG)	Nondurable household products
United Technologies Corporation	(NYSE: UTX)	Aerospace
Verizon Communications	(NYSE: VZ)	Telecoms
Wal-Mart	(NYSE: WMT)	Broadline retailers
Walt Disney	(NYSE: DIS)	Broadcasting & entertainment

Let's say Company B's stock is trading at only $5. If there are also 100,000 shares available, then its market cap is $500,000. Clearly Company A's stock should have a bigger weighting than Company B's.

Thanks to the S&P's market cap calculation, that's exactly what would happen. To find the S&P 500's current value, a computer figures out the total market value of all 500 stocks in the index, adds them together and divides that sum by a number called the "index divisor." In early 2008, the S&P 500 tallied in around 1,353. (Its highest close thus far was 1,565.15 on October 9, 2007, FYI.)

You can see why more people prefer to use the S&P 500 as a market indicator because it gives more of a total market value and includes more stocks from different industries than the Dow. Many mutual fund portfolio managers, for instance, compare their fund's performance with this index.

The Nasdaq Composite   The Nasdaq Composite could be just dubbed the *Tech Index*. Tons of technology companies—including the behemoths like Apple (AAPL), Microsoft (MSFT) and Cisco (CSCO) as well as smaller up-and-comers such as Spectrum Control (SPEC), an electronic-components maker, and American Software (AMSWA), which develops software and services for enterprise management and collaborative supply chains—all trade on the Nasdaq.

The Nasdaq Composite tracks around 5,000 stocks and is calculated just like the S&P 500. The market values of the companies on the Nasdaq are used to calculate the value of the Nasdaq Composite, which in early 2008, rang in around 2,303. Since this index contains so many smaller companies, it offers a good look at that area of the market as well. So many investors use the composite to get an idea of what's going on with the young up-and-comers as well as the tech world.

This index is even more important because over half of all the stocks that are actually traded every day are on the Nasdaq. But critics charge that because the index tracks so many small companies that don't trade as often, it is much more volatile than the others.

A Million Ways to Slice 'n' Dice

Obviously, these are not the only three indexes out there. You can make up an index for just about anything. I'm sure the NFL has indexes that help determine who's going to win the Super Bowl, and I know there's a Paris Hilton index out there that can calculate her next arrest. I just can't find it. So it should come as no surprise that there are over 100 market indexes and averages out there.

Many news and financial services firms have created their own indexes that allow them to slice and dice the market in unique ways. For instance, the Dow Jones Wilshire 5000 Total Stock Market Index represents the stocks of nearly every publicly traded company in the United States, including all U.S. stocks traded on the NYSE and most traded on the Nasdaq and the AMEX. So it's a pretty good total stock market valuation. The FOX 50 is an index that focuses on the largest U.S. companies—such as Starbucks (SBUX), McDonald's (MCD), Exxon (XOM), Home Depot (HD)—that make or sell products you know and use every day. It's a great way to see how the American consumer is doing.

Then there are more specialized indexes that track the performance of specific sectors of the market. The Morgan Stanley Biotech Index, for example, consists of 36 U.S. biotechnology companies.

There are overseas indexes, too. The British FTSE 100, the French CAC 40, the German DAX, the Japanese Nikkei 225, and the Hong Kong Hang Seng Index are the most watched. The Europe, Australia, and Far East Index (EAFE, published by Morgan Stanley) has become hugely popular. It's basically a listing of large companies in the developed economies of the Eastern Hemisphere and since that area is booming, you'll hear that index being quoted all the time.

I'd be remiss if didn't mention the Chicago Board of Options Exchange Volatility Index (VIX). Launched in 2004, the VIX is considered a great barometer of investor sentiment and market volatility. If the VIX is up, that means volatility is on the rise and investors are shaky. (The index is actually based on S&P 500 stock index option prices, but we'll get to options later.) During the market volatility of 2007, the VIX was all over the financial news because it gave pundits an easy way to figure out investor sentiment for the day.

Making Indexes Work for You

So how do you find these indexes? Thanks to our frenetic, obsessive world, these days you can find these numbers just about anywhere. I've seen updates of the broad market indexes on the TV at the dentist office, in elevators, and running across the flat screens at my local coffee shop. (I'm surprised they're not on the bulletin board at my daughter's day care center.) Of course, they're all over the Web. Open up any good financial web site like FOXbusiness.com, WSJ.com, or TheStreet.com, and one of the first things you'll see is the most recent calculation of the Dow, S&P 500, and Nasdaq. I personally have set up my Google home page to show not only the actual numbers of these indexes, but their charts as well.

Of course, no one market index is best for everything. But, let's face it; you're too busy with real life to create the perfect index of your own. So check the Dow, S&P 500, and Nasdaq numbers and you'll quickly get a good idea of what's happening in the entire stock market.

While many will criticize the calculation of the Dow and its representation of the overall, it's still the one index that's been used over time to determine the state of the economy.

Wrap-Up

You now know *what* the market is, *where* it is, and *why* you should be an owner—not an employee—of your favorite company. You can use the market indexes to get an overall sense of what's going. Pull up any financial site—finance.yahoo.com, WSJ.com, TheStreet.com—and the Dow, the S&P 500, and Nasdaq will pop out at you. Those are the numbers people are looking at. You should, too.

Keep in mind that unless you trade for a living, you're in this for the long haul. So if the market is down 200 points one day, don't panic. It's all part of the normal ebb and flow of the business cycle, and history has shown that the markets do go up, even though they may zig and zag along the way. At the beginning of 2008, many would argue that we were in a serious "zag" thanks to the housing slump and the credit issues of the big banks. But the market will work through this just as it worked through the savings and loan crisis of the 1980s, just as it survived the explosion of the tech bubble in the late 1990s and the Enron scandal of the early 2000s. Over the last five years from the beginning of 2008, the Dow was up 54 percent, the S&P 500 was up 62 percent, and the Nasdaq was up a whopping 70 percent.

So trust Gloria Gaynor on this. We will all survive!

2

The Lamborghini Murciélago LP640 Roadster

A LIFETIME OF DIVIDENDS

I want a 2007 Lamborghini Murciélago LP640 Roadster. Preferably while I still have good legs.

I grew up with cars. My uncles are car people. I spent a lot of weekends in parking lots at car shows. My uncle had a 1979 white Corvette with a T-top and I fell in love. From then on, I had a whole new appreciation for the industry.

That's why I love the Lamborghinis so much. Inside and out, they're just genius, and they just keep getting better. The 2007 Murciélago LP640 replaces the 2006 Murciélago coupe. The "LP" stands for *longitudinale posteriore,* which is Italian for "longitudinal rear" and indicates the position of the vehicle's massive V12 engine behind the cockpit in case you care. The number 640 in the name denotes the total horsepower rating of the tweaked V12 engine, up 60 hp from the outgoing Murciélago coupe's V12. Lamborghini says the added power shaves 0.4 seconds from the zero-to-62 mph sprint, bringing it down to a scant 3.4 seconds. Oh sure, someone out there will say there are better, faster, more adeptly engineered cars. Maybe there are, although I doubt it.

I want the Lamborghini. I love those fabulous scissor-action doors, too. Just imagine stepping out of that car. You would have to wear high heels *all* the time. The doors debuted on the groundbreaking Lamborghini Countach in 1973 (again, in case you're interested).

And since I'm factoid girl, most Lamborghinis, including the Murciélago, are named after varieties of Spanish fighting bulls or their breeders. Murciélago was a legendary fighting bull whose life was spared, as the story goes, after valiantly standing up to 24 jabs of a matador's sword in 1879. The bull was given to a breeder, and his descendants are said to be fighting in the ring to this day.

Cool, right?

But the biggest reason I want a Murciélago is that the car pays huge dividends. And since I'm your practical investment girl, I'm all about getting a return on my money.

Let's face it, anyone who drops $300,000 on a car better get something in return. That's the beauty of the Lamborghini. It's the car that keeps on giving. Think about how you'd feel every time you walked out of your house and saw that baby sitting in your driveway.

But then it gets better. You get to gently slip into the cockpit and just take in that dashboard with all its carbon-fiber trim. Keep in mind you haven't even started the car yet and you already have goose bumps. And then you actually get to drive this masterpiece of Italian craftsmanship anywhere you want, anytime you want. (Past my ex-husband's house, preferably.) Even the ride to work takes on a whole new dimension.

Those are your dividends, your rewards for owning the Murciélago. They will last as long as you own the car—and probably long there after as the memories linger on.

Stock dividends offer similar rewards. Clearly, you don't get the same instant gratification with stock dividends as you do with the Lamborghini. And I highly doubt you'll want your picture taken with your new stock dividends. But you do get stock dividends for similar reasons because ownership has its privileges.

When you buy a stock in a company, you become a shareholder and, as a shareholder, you deserve a cut of the company's earnings. That's your dividend for owning the stock. So for the most part, you should look for stocks that offer good dividends.

Of course, just because a company offers a dividend doesn't mean you should go buy it. On the flip side, if your favorite company doesn't pay one, that doesn't mean you should eschew it. You'll need to do some legwork to determine if the dividend is worth it. So let's understand how a company creates a dividend, because we clearly know that a Lamborghini does, and help you decide if it's the right stock for you to own.

The Derivation of Dividend

Dividends are your cut of the company's earnings and are generally paid on a quarterly basis. Once a quarter, you get a check in the mail for the amount of dividends you're entitled to. The amount of the actual dividend can be raised, cut, or eliminated at any time, although once your company gets on the dividend bandwagon, it's very hard to get off. The shareholders and market will not be pleased. Many older shareholders actually live off those dividends checks.

On Wall Street, cutting or eliminating a dividend doesn't send good signals. It basically means the company doesn't have the money to pay the dividend and that doesn't say much about the company's future. General Motors (GM) halved its dividend in February 2006, claiming it needed to wait for profits from its upcoming cars and trucks. Wall Street *still* has no faith in the stock as a result. On the flip side, oil giant Schlumberger (SLB) raised its dividend by 40 percent on January 21, 2007, and the whole oil sector rallied.

So who's responsible for the dividends decisions? The board of directors. A company's board of directors must decide how much money the company will distribute as a dividend.

In an ideal world, a company's business makes tons of money, pays its bills, and has cash left over. Then the board members get to decide how that extra cash is allocated. They can:

- Pay down some of the company's debt.
- Buy back their own shares, which means the company actually goes into the market and buys shares like you and I would.
- Make acquisitions such as land and equipment.
- Give some of it back to you, as your reward for being a shareholder.

There is big motivation for the board to be generous and give back to its shareholders. Remember, Wall Street likes dividends and a steadily increasing dividend payout is viewed as a strong indication of a company's continuing success. So there's a little marketing going on here, too.

Dividends can be anywhere from five cents to a few dollars per share. So if you have 100 shares and the company is giving a 25-cent dividend, you'd get a check for $25 at the end of the quarter. This might not sound like much, but it is money you didn't have before.

The great part about dividends is that they're very black and white. They are paid or not paid, increased or not increased. You either get a reward like driving a car that costs more than your house—or you don't.

That isn't the case with other corporate numbers such as earnings. There's a lot of wiggle room and gray areas with a company's earnings number because it is basically an accountant's "best guess" of a company's profitability. You know how that goes. (Just the name "Enron" evokes thoughts of crooked accounting.). When you're guesstimating, there's plenty of room for creativity in the accounting world. So companies can beef up their earnings numbers to make Wall Street happy. Problems arise when they get caught. Then the company has to go back and redo everything and that creates a mess for investors.

But they can't take back your dividend. It's yours and you're free to do with it as you choose.

Keep in mind that you really don't want to see young companies issuing dividends. If a new company happens to have money
left over, that's impressive However, it should just reinvest that
money back in the business. It should open more stores, increase
marketing, hire more people. Wall Street would expect that.
They would actually frown upon a dividend distribution from a
young company because it had not reinvested to strengthen its
position for the long haul. So for the most part, you're looking
for dividends from companies that have been around the track a
few times.

Dissecting a Dividend's Date

Now that you know how fabulous dividends are, you need to
know how to get them. So make sure you know the actual date
of the big giveaway.

I can't tell you how many times I've shown up at a store,
ready to purchase stuff I can't afford, only to have the sales-
person tell me that the store is having a "20%-off sale" starting
tomorrow. The rest of the conversation goes something like this:

"But I'm here *today*."

"Can you come back tomorrow?"

"No. That's why I'm here today."

She should've said, "Thanks, sucker," as I signed the receipt
for full price.

To avoid this situation, you need to know the date of the
big giveaway.

There are four major dates that are part of the dividend
process, but, in a nutshell, you need to be a shareholder of the
company on the date of record to qualify for the dividend:

1. The *declaration date* is the date the board announces to
   the world that it's giving a free gift to shareholders.
2. The *ex-date, ex-div,* or *ex-dividend date* is the first day that
   your stock will trade without its dividend. ("Ex" is Latin
   for "without.") This means if you buy the stock one
   day before the ex-dividend, you'll still get the dividend

because you're buying a stock that still has a dividend. If you buy the stock on the ex-div date, you're out.

3. The *date of record* is that day the company looks at to determine who gets the dividend. It basically opens up its shareholder roster. If you're on it, you win. If you're not, better luck next time.

4. The *date of payment* is basically the date the company mails out the dividend checks.

If you're a long-term investor and plan on holding your dividend-paying stock for a while, these dates aren't all that important because you'll be a shareholder of record without a problem. But if you're thinking of selling or buying the stock close to the ex-dividend date, get out your PDA because you need to be a shareholder on the day of record to get that dividend. Even in this technological age, it still takes three days from the day you buy the shares to get you on the company's shareholder roster. Traders call this the *T + 3 settlement process.* If you buy a stock today, it'll be another three days before your name ends up on the company's shareholder books.

If you are not in the company's record books on the date of record, you won't receive the dividend payment. To ensure that you are in the record books, buy the stock at least three days before the date of record.

Let's say Monday morning, your favorite company announces a big $2 dividend and you want to be a part of it. The date of record is Thursday, so you'll need to buy shares on Monday to get the dividend. If you wait until Tuesday, you won't be a shareholder on record until Friday. That means no dividend.

Of course, before you get to *when* you'll receive your dividend check, you first need to decide if you *want* it. Just because someone is giving out free samples of Sean Combs's (a.k.a. P. Diddy, Sean "Puffy" Combs, etc.) new fragrance *Unforgivable,* doesn't necessarily mean you're going to smell good in it. So don't just dive in because the company is offering a dividend. Do some legwork first.

Rev the Engine with Some Ratios

Here's where we need to do a little research, so log on to Yahoo! Finance (or your favorite financial web site), put in your company's ticker, and click on the "Key Statistics" section. Let's look at Merck (MRK), a company notorious for paying a super dividend.

First look at the *dividend payout ratio*. It's just dividends per share divided by *earnings per share* (EPS). It basically tells you what percentage of earnings is coming back to you. If you got a $1 dividend and EPS is $3, the payout ratio is 33 percent. That means you're getting 33 percent of the good stuff. Not bad. In December 2007, Merck was giving out 62 percent of the pot. Yeah baby!

Of course, this ratio means nothing in isolation, so you need to compare to it to other companies in the same industry. So drop in some competitors' tickers and go to the key statistics section again. For instance, Johnson & Johnson's (JNJ) dividend payout was 45 percent in December 2007. Still not too shabby.

So be sure to compare to its peers. If your company's dividend yield is 33 percent but the rest of its peers are giving out 45 percent, your 33 percent doesn't look so pretty anymore.

Next, move on to the *dividend yield*. That's just the annual dividend per share divided by the stock's price. It essentially gives you the return on your investment. Say two companies both pay an annual dividend of $1 per share. Your company's dividend yield is 2.5 percent, but its competitor is yielding 5 percent. So you get a better return on your investment with the competitor.

That's why it's important to look at the competition.

Drive through the Financials

I know you'd rather read *Cosmopolitan* or *Car and Driver* than a company's financial statements. But if you're going to play this game, you've got to play it right and play to win.

Pull out your company's financials and read the president's letter and management's discussion and analysis. (We'll get into that in more detail in Chapter 5.) Companies that offer dividends are pretty proud of it, so you'll probably find some mention of it here. If the company has initiated a dividend for the first time, stand back—you might actually hear music. Check out the excerpt from Citigroup's 2006 annual report:

> The Board of Directors increased the quarterly common dividend by 11% during 2006 and by an additional 10% in January 2007, bringing the current quarterly payout to $0.54 per share.

But good news is often short lived as we all know. This is exactly why you need to stay on top of your stocks. While this dividend news was stellar at the beginning of the year, by January 2008, the company had *cut* its dividend by *41 percent* to meet its struggling financial needs as a result of the credit crisis. The stock is down over 50 percent since it bragged about its stellar dividend in its 2006 annual report. Boo, Citigroup.

Next, flip to the cash flow statement (which we'll dissect further in Chapter 7). The company has to have cash before it can distribute it to you. So be sure you see positive numbers in the "operating cash" section, with preferably an increase over the last few years.

Finally, look at the long-term debt number on the balance sheet. Is it increasing? If the company owes too much, the dividend might be the first thing to go if they have bills to pay.

It's All About the Little Things

With investing, like luxury sports cars, the little things count. To go back to my Murciélago, not only has the overall mechanics of the car been taken to the next level, but the interior has as well. The seats are more spacious and, therefore, more comfortable. And the leather upholstery now features this lozenge-shaped stitching called *Q-citura*. The stitching is repeated on the upholstery of the door panels, the panel between the seats and the engine compartment, even on the roof panel. It's gorgeous.

These little details just add so much to the overall picture. That's exactly why I love dividends. Those little checks can really make a difference to your overall portfolio.

But take note: they can be little. Dividends can be as little as 10 cents a share. Some companies, such as Altria (MO), offer a $5 annual dividend, but for the most part it's generally around $1 per year. For instance, if you own one share of Coca-Cola (KO), you're quarterly dividend check would be around 38 cents.

It might not sound like much, but what if you owned 150 shares of Coke? Your dividend check would jump to $57. That's practically enough money to buy another share of Coke, which was trading around $58 at the beginning of 2008. So you just got a share of stock for free.

Think of dividends like emptying your spare change into a jar every night. Before you know it, there's $100 in there and you just bought yourself a fabulous new pair of shoes to match your Lamborghini. So look for companies that not only offer a dividend, but also keep increasing it over the years. Take an all-American stock like Harley-Davidson (HOG). Not only has the stock price been growing consistently, but the company has increased its dividend consecutively for the last 12 years. Or check out a company like Paychex (PAYX). The company has consecutively increased its dividend over the last 18 years and the stock is up over 5,000 percent over that time!

So look for good companies that continue to increase their dividends over the years. Those stocks will help keep your portfolio on track during market booms and busts. According to Mergent, Inc., which tracks business and financial performance, the following are four companies that have steadily increased their dividends over the last 10 years:

- Harley-Davidson, Inc. (NYSE: HOG)
- Home Depot, Inc. (NYSE: HD)
- Paychex (Nasdaq: PAYX)
- Lehman Brothers Holdings, Inc. (NYSE: LEH)
- Cardinal Health, Inc. (NYSE: CAH)

There is one small downside. Those dividend distributions, however small they may be, are considered taxable income to you. That means you must report them on your tax return and pay Uncle Sam his fair share. (Did you actually think he was going to let you get a freebie?) It's annoying, but even after Uncle Sam's cut, those little dividends are still worth it.

Get To Know a DRIP (Dividend Reinvestment Program)

Now you know what a stock is and why a company gives its shareholders a dividend (and more importantly, why you deserve it). When a company pays a dividend, it cuts you a check and mails it home to you unless otherwise notified. So here's the big question:

What are you doing with those quarterly dividend checks?
Are you:

A. Cashing them and going out for dinner?
B. Cashing them and hitting the shoe sale?
C. Reinvesting them?

If you picked A or B, you and I will be friends for life because we are clearly on the same wavelength. But wait! You're not reading this book to make friends with me.

What you should be doing is answer C. As boring as it sounds, your portfolio will thank me. Reinvesting dividends can make you serious money—I'll show you why in a minute. The best way to reinvest those dividends is to sign up for the company's *dividend reinvestment program* (DRIP).

So let's dissect the DRIP.

What's a DRIP?

A dividend reinvestment plan is a way for shareholders to reinvest their dividends back into the company. Instead of getting those dividend checks sent home, the company just keeps the money and buys more shares for you.

Reinvesting your dividends can make a huge difference in the amount of shares you hold over the long haul. You could end up with as many as *two or three times* as many shares as you started with. Let's say you invested $2,000 in PepsiCo (PEP) back in 1980. You should have started with 80 shares. Presuming you had all your dividends reinvested back into the stock, by the end of 2006, you'd have 2,800 shares worth around $150,000. I swear!

Try it with Altria—the old Philip Morris—$2,000 in 1980 bought you about 58 shares. Thanks to reinvesting dividends and stock splits (see Sometimes, Even Stocks Need to Split), you had 4,300 shares by the end of 2006, valued at around $140,000.

Sometimes, Even Stocks Need to Split

All public companies have a set number of shares that are outstanding—or available—on the stock market. But there are times when the company's board of directors feels it's necessary to increase the number of available shares.

That's when a *stock split* occurs. Then the share you hold is "split" into more shares. Here's an example. If you own one share, in a two-for-one stock split you will have two shares after the split. If a company had 10 million shares outstanding before the split, it will now have 20 million shares outstanding after a two-for-one split. Keep in mind the stock's price is split as well. In our example of a two-for-one split, the share price will be halved. If you spent $100 on a single share before the split, you now have two shares worth $50 each.

Splits usually happen to drum up demand for the shares. Often companies think the share price has gotten too high and so if they split them, and decrease the price, the shares might seem more affordable.

The opposite of a stock split is a *reverse split*. Companies use reverse splits when they think the share price is too low and are looking to gain some more respectability in the market. So in a reverse five-for-one split, 10 million outstanding shares at 50 cents each would now become 2 million shares outstanding at $2.50 per share. In both cases, the company is worth $50 million.

It's a bit of smoke and mirrors, don't you think?

Here's another upside: Since you're buying the shares directly from the company, there are *no broker fees* for the purchase. Remember, typically when you buy a stock, you have to pay your broker a small fee for shuffling some paper around and executing the trade. Well, when you reinvest your dividends, the company is handling the transaction, so there's no middle man, and in turn, no extra fees. Yippee!

Beware, though. Even though you're no longer getting those checks in the mail, those reinvested distributions are still taxable income to you. Can't escape Uncle Sam.

Usually, you need to own just one share of the company to be a part of its DRIP, though every company's different. PepsiCo, for example, requires five shares to enroll. So check with your company. But it's still such a small amount. That's why I think everyone should start giving little kids shares of stock for special occasions. My stepbrother gave my daughter a few shares of Coca-Cola when she was a baby. I reinvest the dividends for her and, although she's only three, she's got quite a portfolio.

Of Course, the Company Benefits, Too

Of course, my delicious little girl is not the only one benefiting from these DRIP plans. Clearly, there are perks to the companies that offer these plans or they wouldn't bother.

To start, the company has immediate access to your money when you reinvest. When you buy a share on the open market, you're essentially buying it from another seller. With a DRIP, you purchase right from the company so your money is immediately in their hands.

In addition, companies like the solid shareholder base. If you're a DRIP investor, you're pretty wedded to the company. If the market goes down or a negative one-time event happens, you wouldn't be as quick to jump ship as someone who didn't have as much of a vested interest in the place.

Take AFLAC (AFL), the company that sells supplemental life insurance policies and has that hilarious duck in its commercials. With 64 percent of its shareholders participating in its DRIP, the company's got a ton of loyal shareholders that probably aren't leaving any time soon. Its plan is one of the best and has been around since 1973. In early 2008, AFLAC paid a quarterly dividend of 24 cents a share.

RPM, a Fortune 500 specialty chemical company, claims that 71 percent of its shareholders are enrolled in its DRIP, which has been in existence since 1969, according to DividendInvestor .com. RPM's 2008 quarterly dividend was 19 cents.

So How Do You Find a DRIP?

Let me give you my ex-husband's address. Forgive me, I've been biting my tongue since I started writing this part of the chapter.

There are about 1,600 companies offering DRIPs these days, so first figure out if the company you're investigating is one of them. Go to the investor relations section of its web site or check out stock sites, such as StockSelector.com, that list companies with DRIPs.

Next, make sure you're a shareholder in your DRIP company and that you hold the minimum amount of shares necessary to participate. DRIPs can vary from company to company. Some companies only let you buy new shares based on the amount of dividends you're reinvesting. Others allow you to add some cash and buy more shares. So do some legwork and make sure you understand the plan.

Then you have a few choices.

You could buy the shares directly through the company. Fill out the paperwork and *voila!* You're a DRIP member. But remember, you'll then have to track all those purchases because you'll need to know the price that you paid for those few shares. Then, when you decide to sell those shares, you'll be able to calculate your profits. That could get onerous because every time your dividends are reinvested, you'll have a new lot of shares to keep track of. So you'll need to keep a spreadsheet of every purchase. Be sure to include the share price you paid and the date of purchase, so you know your cost basis when you decide to sell those shares someday.

Or you can just use the Internet. Following are some web sites that will track your dividend repurchases for you:

- GainsKeeper.com
- ShareBuilder.com
- MyStockFund.com

A better option might be to set up your DRIP through your brokerage account. Most Web-based brokers allow you to reinvest your dividends for no charge—so you don't have to go through the company. For instance, ShareBuilder.com and MyStockFund.com will let you reinvest for free. Then you'll have all your trades under one roof.

One caveat: You may need the stock certificates (as archaic as that sounds) issued in your name to qualify for the DRIP through your broker. So be sure to check that out.

Most DRIPs are pretty flexible and allow you to make periodic cash investments. The amount can be as little as $10 or as much as $100,000 in one shot. I just sent a check for $50 to my daughter's account. And again, most of these cash purchases are commission free.

Even better, some DRIPs offer the shares at a slight discount to the current market price. Discounts can range from as little as 1 percent to as much as 10 percent. When combined with no commission fees, you end up paying a lot less for those shares than you would if you bought them through your broker.

All very good.

DRIP Downers

While DRIPs allow you to add to your position without incurring onerous fees, there is some downside:

- *Most DRIPs decide what day your new shares will be purchased— usually once a month.* So if you're a short-term trader, trying to buy on the dips, this might not work for you. This isn't an issue for a long-term investor, though.

- *Same goes for selling those shares.* You can sell only on certain days. So if you're trying to get out of a stock because of bad news, it might not be so easy. Again, not a problem for the long-term investor.
- *Watch the fees.* There may be extraneous fees just for being involved in the DRIP. Stay away from those plans. Try to invest only in DRIPs that don't charge you anything extra.
- You need to *hone your record keeping.* If you're in the stock for the long haul, you could have hundreds of dividend purchases. So create a spreadsheet that tracks all those trades or use a program that tracks your trades for you, like GainsKeeper.com. Otherwise, see if you can participate in the DRIP through your broker. Then your trades will be under one roof.
- Just because you don't get the checks doesn't mean you don't owe the tax. Cash was distributed to you. You just opted to have it reinvested back in the stock. So those distributions, whether they're 50 cents or $500, are still taxable income to you and you must report them on your tax return. You will then owe tax on them (The rate could be as low as 15 percent on ordinary dividends, but that's always subject to change.)

Despite all this, I still think a DRIP could still be a cheap way to amp up your position.

Wrap-Up

Once you've found a good company that you want to own, check out its dividend history. Ideally you want to see a long history of increasing dividends. Companies like Johnson & Johnson and 3M are perfect examples. Solid companies with at least a decade of increasing dividends are good places to start. Table 2.1 shows some of the best-performing dividend stocks over time.

Table 2.1   Some of Best-Performing Dividend Stocks in Early 2008

Stock	Annual Dividend Yield
Anheuser-Busch (NYSE: BUD)	2.8%
Hershey (NYSE: HSY)	3.2%
Chevron (NYSE:CVX)	2.7%
VF (NYSE: VFC)	2.9%
McDonald's (NYSE: MCD)	2.7%
AFLAC (NYSEAFL)	1.5%

Source: Yahoo! Finance.

Then investigate its DRIP program. Hopefully there are no extraneous fees for participating.

Finally, sign up, sit back, and watch your money grow. Those little dividends have the potential to make you pretty happy over time.

Much like that Murciélago that should be sitting in my driveway.

CHAPTER 3

Bond, James Bond

How can you not love James Bond? He's the ultimate man. I adored Sean Connery as James Bond in the 1964 movie *Goldfinger* ("Just a drink—a martini—shaken, not stirred."), and Daniel Craig was pretty juicy as the new Bond in *Casino Royale*.

Unfortunately, the bonds that trade in the financial markets are not nearly as sexy. But if you're going to understand the markets, you've got to understand bonds. Let's face it, you can't read an economic report these days with having to get through some bond market data.

One day, on the way to work, I heard a pundit say:

> Treasuries were inching higher. The 10-year note was up 2/32 in price, yielding 4.63 percent, and the 30-year bond was adding 2/32, yielding 4.82 percent.

What?

The bond market, though generally an enigma to most investors, is quite correlated to the equities market. As Frank Sinatra croons in *Love and Marriage*, "You can't have one without the other."

So we have no choice but to talk bond basics:

- James Bond 007 is a fictional British secret agent created in 1952 by writer Ian Fleming.
- Roger Moore played James Bond in seven films, a record.
- Ursula Andress as Honey Ryder in *Dr. No* was the hottest Bond girl, hands-down. (Sorry, Halle.)

Oops, not those basics. Read on!

Bond with the Family

There are a bunch of similar concepts among all bonds, so let's illustrate with a very commonplace example.

Your brother needs a $5,000 loan. You have no desire to loan him money because you know you'll never see it again. But this time he gets smart and offers you an 8 percent semiannual interest payment on your loan. He swears on his custom-made motorcycle (no, I am not speaking from experience) that he'll repay your $5,000 in three years. For some unknown reason, you decide to give him the benefit of the doubt and loan him the $5,000. In addition, you set up an automatic debit from his checking account to yours (because you got smart, too) for your $200 semiannual interest payment. Annual interest would be $400—8 percent on $5,000—but you need to divide it over two payments. So every six months you automatically got your interest payments and, sure enough, three years later you also got back your $5,000. Apparently, he wasn't willing to part with his bike.

That's basically how the bond market works, without the motorcycle. If you buy a bond, you're essentially loaning the issuer of the bond some money. He will then pay you some interest, usually twice a year, as your bonus for loaning him money.

Now, no matter what kind of bond you buy, they all have a few commonalities. Every bond has a "face value," which is the principal portion of the loan. These days, it's either $1,000 or $5,000. That's also the amount you generally pay up front for the bond, and it's the amount you'll get back from the issuer on the day your loan is over.

When your loan ends, the bond folks say your bond has *matured*. (Just like your brother.) Let's say you buy a 10-year bond with a $5,000 face value. Your bond will come due, or mature, 10 years from the day it was issued. On that final day, you'll get your $5,000 back. These days, maturities can be as long as 30 years or as short as 3 years.

The interest you get on that bond is sometimes called your *coupon payment*. Years ago, bonds used to come with attached coupons that investors had to clip so they could redeem their interest payments. These days, it's all done electronically. But old habits die hard, so that interest payment is still called the *coupon*.

A bond with an 8 percent coupon pays 8 percent interest based on the face value of the bond in two semiannual installments. Assuming a face value of $5,000, like in our example above, that's two $200 interest payments a year.

The Mature Bond

Some people assume that because bonds have maturity dates, they're pretty much guaranteed investments. That's true in most instances. It's no surprise that older investors who need secured money for retirement invest in bonds. Same goes for the guy how knows his kid will be in college in five years or has a child getting married in the near future. When you know you need the money soon, you sometimes don't want to risk it in the stock market. Remember, everyone is eating fat-free pizza now and your YUM! investment is doing well, but the fat-free fried chicken at KFC may end up tasting like shoe leather. Then, no doubt, the stock will tank.

As much as bonds are supposed to be the stable, low-risk portion of your portfolio, the world of bond investing is still rife with pitfalls. That's because bonds have credit risk. If the U.S. government issues you a bond, a Treasury bond, then you can rest assured that you're going to get your money back. But if you decide to buy a bond from a risky company because it's offering a really high interest payment, you run the risk that the company is not going to have the money to give back to you when your bond matures.

Bonds also have interest-rate risk—no surprise. Let's say you bought a bond with a 6 percent interest payment. But what if interest rates rise? Now there are bonds out there with 8 percent interest rates. So you're missing out on a higher interest payment.

That's why bonds with longer maturities, such as 10-year and 30-year bonds, have more interest-rate risk. The odds are good that interest rates will change over 10 years. But if you buy a bond that has a one-year maturity, the rates probably won't change that much during that 12-month period.

So you have to analyze two things: 1) whether the issuer is going to be able to pay you in the end and 2) whether you're interest rate risk is too much to handle.

A Bond's Yield

One final piece of jargon you need to be aware of: a bond's *yield*. In general, the yield of anything is its annual rate of return, expressed as a percentage. A bond's yield is essentially the value of its interest payments. That's your annual cash inflows divided by the price of your investment shown as a percentage.

We need an example. Let's say you buy a $1,000 bond with a 5 percent interest, or coupon, rate. That means you'll receive an annual payment of $50. That's pretty straightforward.

But not all bonds sell at face value. Bond prices oftentimes change when stock prices change. If a company comes out with bad earnings or makes an announcement that causes the stock to fall, its bond's price will slip too. So in our example, let's presume that you're looking at a bond whose price has fallen to $800. Now, how do you determine its yield?

Divide your payments by your price (50/800 × 100). In our example, your $800 bond is yielding 6.25 percent. That lower price actually increases your rate of return. In other words, the price and the yield are inversely proportional. The yield goes up when the price goes down and vice versa—6.25 percent ends up in your wallet instead of 5 percent.

Yippee!

Now that you know how to calculate a bond's yield, use it as a good basis of comparison with other bonds. Keep in mind that higher-yield bonds generally come with more risk. That's because the issuer knows that there's a chance it may default on the loan or that the bond's maturity is a long way off. So the issuer pays you more in the form of an interest payment for taking a chance and helping him with its debt.

And speaking of a "Bond's" yield, one more factoid: If you inflation-adjust the total box office sales of the 21 Bond films (*Bond 22* is coming out in 2008), the 1965 *Thunderball* was the highest grosser at $886,994,986. *Goldfinger* came in second with $794,800,903 in sales. And *Casino Royale* ranked seventh with $594,293,106.

No surprise, Mr. Connery was in the top two.

Wrap-Up

So now you've got some bond lingo down. You understand that while bonds are usually considered a "safe" investment because you are, in most instances, guaranteed an income stream, they come with some risk: The issuer might not be able to cover the loan and the interest rates in the market may change.

More importantly, you're now armed with some fabulous James Bond trivia that you can pull out at the next cocktail party.

4

Mutual Funds and ETFs

FOR FOLKS ON THE GO

Owning stocks and bonds can make you serious money if you have the opportunity to analyze them and pick good ones. But many of us just don't have that kind of time. Between little Johnny's T-ball games, trying to get to the gym, and that pesky presentation at work, we don't even have a chance to reheat dinner, let alone pick individual stocks. Mutual funds and exchange-traded funds are a great way to get exposure to the markets with a lot less effort.

Mutual Funds: Funds for Kegs

As an undergrad, I went to Lehigh University in Bethlehem, Pennsylvania. There were 32 fraternities and a mere 8 sororities when I was there. (No need to discuss the guy-girl ratio.) With the Greek system comes a fair amount of beer drinking. Milwaukee's Best was the beer of choice when I was there. Keystone was our treat when someone had extra money, but no one ever did. We would pool our money and get kegs. Everyone would pitch in $5 and a leader would be chosen to drive off into the sunset and hopefully return with the goods. Pooling our money for a keg was way more efficient than going out and buying individual six-packs. See, we were industrious students.

Believe it or not, mutual funds work in the same way. Investors pool their money, put someone in charge of trading stocks or bonds, and get cheaper prices for buying in bulk. Bet you never thought that all those years of scraping up beer money were actually teaching you a valuable lesson!

Think of your mutual fund as, dare I say, a keg of stocks.

A mutual fund is simply a portfolio of stocks, bonds, or both. Most mutual funds are *actively managed,* which means a fund manager is hired to make all the buy/sell decisions. You send your money to the fund, and the manager decides how to invest it. Just as you trusted that your buddy would not drive off with your beer money, you have to trust that your fund manager is going to make smart decisions. That's why you have to believe in your manager's track record.

These days, it's tough to be a manager. Take former New York Yankees manager Joe Torre. He had a killer winning streak until the 2006 season, when he was practically guillotined. Meanwhile, Torre got his 2,000th win on June 7, 2007, and became the first major league manager to win 2,000 games and have 2,000 hits. But New York baseball fans have very high standards, and after the season Torre was off the Yankee payroll in spite of his track record. (The Los Angeles Dodgers seemed to still have faith in him and hired him as the team's new manager.) Mutual fund investors have similar standards. Make money for the team, or get out!

Obviously, fund managers don't work for free. Nor does Joe Torre. You'll have to pay a yearly fee for your manager's services as well. We'll delve into these fees more in a bit, but basically, you need to make sure your manager is worth his fee. (Was Torre worth $6.3 million? Is anyone?)

A mutual fund is legally known as an *open-end investment company.* The "open-end" part basically means you can sell your shares and get your money at a price based on the current value of the fund's net assets at any time. The "company" part means you become a shareholder when you buy into the mutual fund. Each piece of the fund that you purchase is called a share.

And just like a stock, you can purchase shares directly from the fund company or through your broker.

First, the Good News: Perks

You just can't beat an ice-cold beer at a summer barbeque. Especially if it's Pete's Summer Brew (one of my favorites). Even better, beer has no fat or cholesterol, and is a source of soluble fiber. Yep. A liter of beer contains an average of 20 percent of the recommended daily intake of fiber and some beers can provide up to 60 percent. I'm not kidding. See, it's good for you!

Mutual funds can also be very good for a healthy portfolio. Arguably one of the best investments ever created, they're very cost-efficient and simple to invest in (remember, you don't have to figure out which stocks or bonds to buy—that's your manager's job). In addition, by pooling money together in a mutual fund, investors purchase stocks or bonds at much lower trading costs than if they tried to do it on their own. It's that whole "buy-in-bulk" thing—exactly why I shop at Costco (COST).

The biggest advantage to buying mutual funds, though, is the ability to diversify with one purchase. With each share, you'll get a piece of every holding in the fund.

Here's a *very* simple example. Let's say you decide to buy into a fund that has three stocks—shares of Coca-Cola (KO), Yum! Brands (YUM), and Budweiser (BUD). So if you buy one share of the fund, you'll essentially own 1 share of the Coke, 1 share of Yum!, and 1 share of Bud. You just got exposure to three stocks all for the price of one.

Now here's the diversification perk. Let's presume people decide that beer makes you fat after all and they start drinking Diet Coke at barbeques instead. Budweiser will start to sell less beer so the value of your Budweiser share will decline. That's a bummer because you own a share of that stock through your mutual fund purchase. On the flip side, Coca-Cola will benefit from this new skinny fad and will sell more Diet Coke. Coke shares will go up and you'll be happy again because you own that stock, too. So by owning one share in that mutual fund, you've covered yourself.

Now you could diversify on your own with individual stocks. But then you would have to monitor them, make sure they're doing well, and decide when it's time to sell. Who has time for that? I can barely braid my daughter's hair and get her to school on time, let alone find an hour to myself to read Coca-Cola's financial statements. I'm not sure which one is more tedious.

However, if you buy into one good mutual fund, you own everything with one purchase.

A History Lesson: Two Time-Honored Traditions

Beer is one of the oldest human-produced beverages, possibly dating back to the 7th millennium BCE, in ancient Egypt and Mesopotamia. The earliest known chemical evidence of beer dates to circa 3500–3100 BCE. Imagine the pharaohs having beers. Gives a whole to meaning to "Walk Like an Egyptian."

Granted, mutual funds are not nearly as old. But modern man has been investing in them since 1924, when the first fund was created by the Massachusetts Investors Trust with 45 stocks and $50,000 in assets. Within the first year, the Trust grew to $392,000 in assets (with around 200 shareholders). The stock market crash of 1929 slowed the growth of mutual funds, but by the end of the 1960s there were around 270 funds with $48 billion in assets.

Today there are over 10,000 mutual funds in the United States today, with 83 million individual investors pooling about $7 trillion, according to the Investment Company Institute.

Fermentations and Permutations

There are about 25 styles of beer and about 70 substyles, according to the Beer Judge Certification Program. This includes anything from a pale ale to a lager to the watered-down stuff we drank at Lehigh.

While mutual funds come in tons of "fermentations" as well, there are a few overriding categories. We'll explore them—stock funds, bond funds, balanced funds, international funds, sector funds, index funds—in the rest of this section.

Keep in mind, however, that just because a fund falls into a particular category or has a particular investment style doesn't mean 100 percent of the fund has to follow that philosophy. You could buy a so-called "stock fund" that only has to have 60 percent of its money in stocks. The remaining money can be invested in bonds or just held in cash. That's why you have to read the fine print.

Stock Funds   These funds invest primarily in stocks or *equities*. That means your fund manager will buy shares of publicly traded companies.

There are tons of stock funds available these days so it is the biggest—and most confusing—category in the fund world. Basically, a stock or equity fund invests in publicly traded companies.

A mutual fund's overall investment philosophy determines the kind of stocks the manager will buy. There are many great funds that invest in the market as a whole. Funds like Vanguard's Total Stock Market Index (VTSMX) and the Fidelity Spartan Total Market Index (FSTMX) are great representations of the overall market.

Other funds have more specific strategies or investment philosophies. For instance, a growth fund will purchase shares of companies that have good growth potential. A value fund will invest in companies the manager believes are a good value. He believes the stocks are cheap relative to their earning potential. (For more on growth and value stocks, see Chapter 9.)

Stock funds can be further broken down by the market capitalization, or *market cap*, of a company. That's simply the value of the company on the stock market, which is the number of outstanding shares of the company times the price of those shares. For example, if a company has 50 million shares outstanding and each share is currently trading at $100 (its market value), the company's market capitalization is $50 billion (50,000,000 × $100 per share).

There are three main types of "cap" funds: large cap, mid-cap, and small cap. Large-cap funds tend to invest in companies with market caps above $10 billion; midcap funds tend to invest in companies with market caps of $1 billion to $10 billion; and small-cap funds tend to invest in companies with market caps below $1 billion.

Some mutual funds also add a fourth category called *micro-cap* funds to describe funds that invest in companies worth less than $250 million. In general, the smaller the average market cap of the fund's holdings, the more volatile the return. Microcap funds can be especially risky.

This additional "cap" permutation means you could invest in a small-cap growth fund or a large-cap value fund.

Bond Funds   Bond mutual funds invest in—you guessed it—bonds.

Generally called *fixed income funds,* there are fewer incarnations of bond funds. They are mostly differentiated by maturities. If the manager is buying bonds that come due 5 to 10 years from now, it would be considered more of a long-term bond fund. If she's buying short-term notes that come due in six months, it would be a short-term fund.

We talked about how bonds give off an interest—or coupon—payment. When you own a bond fund, you still get that interest payment. The difference is that your payment will be your corresponding piece of the interest from all the bonds in the fund.

Balanced Funds   Balanced funds are some combination of stocks and bonds. It's usually around 50/50, but again that could change depending on the philosophy of the fund.

International Funds   International funds invest in companies whose headquarters are not in the United States. International funds tend to be much riskier than U.S.-based funds for a few reasons: The United States is the most stable economy in the world, so everything else pales in comparison, and it's much harder to understand what's going on in another country.

Sector Funds   Sector funds take a bet on one particular sector of the economy such as technology, banking, alcohol, or oil. They can be a riskier investment for you because you're gambling on a particular segment of the market. Just because the Vice Fund (VICEX), which owns companies like Heineken and Diageo (the maker of Johnny Walker scotch and Captain Morgan rum), is rocketing today, you're presuming that everyone is going to keep drinking in the future. (That doesn't seem like much of a gamble.)

Because of this, you need to pay very close attention to your sector funds. Just because oil is hot today, doesn't mean that someone won't come up with some ground-breaking substitute in the near future and oil then will be used only for salads.

Index Funds   Oftentimes, beer drinkers are presumed to be out-of-shape couch potatoes who get the shakes if the remote is more than six inches away. If that's true, then they will love index funds. Some call them the lazy man's funds, but they are some of my favorites because they are the easiest way to invest in the market.

An index mutual fund mirrors one of the market's many different broader indexes. So a Standard & Poor's 500 Composite Stock Price Index (S&P 500) fund owns a piece of each of the 500 companies listed in the S&P. You can't get any more diversified than that.

John Bogle, the founder of the Vanguard Group, opened the first index fund in 1976 and it was called, not coincidentally, the First Index Investment Trust. Today, it's the Vanguard 500 Index Fund and probably the most well-known fund available. In November 2000, it became the largest mutual fund ever, with $100 billion in assets.

Because these mutual funds just follow a market index— like the S&P 500, the Nasdaq, or the Russell 100, to name a few—it doesn't take a whole lot to run these funds. The managers just make sure the fund mirrors its particular index and they can go back to playing Halo 3 on their office Xbox. Since they're not doing a "ton" of work, you shouldn't have to pay those fund managers as much as the managers of your regular stock or bond funds—which brings us back to the fees.

Now the Bad News

Clearly, beer isn't all that good for us. Table 4.1 says so. Alcohol interferes with the body's absorption of vitamins and minerals and can lessen the body's ability to burn stored fat. What's worse, calories from alcohol most likely go right to your stomach. How's this for an annoying scientific factoid: In the process of metabolizing excess quantities of alcohol, the liver swells and may become filled with fat. That's another reason why you end up with a "beer belly" after slugging a six-pack.

Thankfully, investing in mutual funds doesn't affect your waist size. They do have an annoying darker side, though, and it's all in the fees that you have to pay to be a part of this pool.

We talked before about how you have to pay your manager to pick good stocks. But here's the sad reality: Approximately 80 percent of mutual funds underperform the average return of the stock market. So all the MBAs you pay to pick great stocks in your mutual fund are not really doing all that well

Table 4.1 Nutritional Value of Beer

Brewery/Brand	Beer	Alcohol(%)	Calories	Carbs
Miller	Miller Genuine Draft	5.0	143	13.1
Miller	Miller Genuine Draft Lite	4.2	110	7.0
Miller	Miller High Life	5.5	156	11.0
Miller	Miller Lite	4.2	96	3.2
Sierra Nevada	Sierra Nevada Bigfoot	9.9	330	30.3
Budweiser (U.S)	Budweiser	5.0	143	10.6
Budweiser	Bud Light	4.2	95	6.6

Source: Realbeer.com.

after all. Why? Because not only does your fund manager have to be smart enough to beat the market, he (or she) has to beat it by enough to cover his management fee as well. If he isn't, you're better off doing it by yourself.

Mutual funds charge shareholders a bunch of little fees that many people just blindly pay. But friends don't let friends pay extraneous fees. In the next section are some of the fees the industry tries to pawn off on unknowing investors.

The Loads

Let's begin with what the industry calls a *load*. A load is basically a chunk of money that a broker or other adviser pays to himself or his company for telling you to buy that fund. Clearly, he has a vested interest in selling you the funds that he's going to get a kickback on. So be wary.

No-load funds are sold directly to the investor rather than through a middleman. If you want to buy a Vanguard fund, you can call Vanguard directly. Brokers such as Charles Schwab and Fidelity also offer no-load funds. So there's no need to pay a sales charge if you have your account with them.

As I said, there are tons of no-load funds available, so there is rarely a reason to buy a fund with any kind of a load. But just so you know, here is how these unnecessary fees work: A *front-end load* is a fee charged the minute you send your money into the fund. It's on the "front end" of your purchase. Front-end loads are typically around 5 percent of your investment; but I've seen them go as high as 8 percent. Let's say you decided to invest $1,000 in a fund with a 5 percent front-end load. Right off the bat, $50 is immediately taken out of your investment and put into the broker's pocket. So you've really invested only $950. That stinks.

Back-end loads (also known as *deferred loads* or *contingent deferred sale loads*—CDSLs) are just as awful except that they defer the pain until you sell your shares in the fund. I remember getting burned when I first started investing. I bought the Fidelity Select Electronics (FSELX) fund and my investment practically doubled inside of a month. I was fired up! I was still married at the time and decided to take my winnings and dump them into our new house. So I sold the shares. I was doing the happy dance and started picking out fabric for window treatments. But when the sale came through and the final number was in front of me, I almost threw up on that silk tapestry fabric I picked for the family room. There was a back-end load on the fund! I was livid. I clearly had no one to blame but myself because I obviously didn't read the fine print. Why would a financial journalist with an MBA do that? That back-end fee took a big chunk out of my earnings.

The moral of this story is: Don't buy a fund with a load. I never did get those window treatments.

Other Fees and Expenses

In addition to those potential loads, most funds charge fees and expenses to cover the fund's overhead. The costs of record keeping, mailings, maintaining a customer service line, and so on. are all necessary business expenses and as a shareholder, you have to help pay for them. (Kind of like chipping in for gas money when your buddy goes to pick up the keg.) These administrative fees vary from fund to fund. The thriftiest funds can keep these costs below 0.20 percent of fund assets, while the ones that use engraved paper and offer free lattes in the lunch room to employees might have administrative costs that come close to 0.40 percent of fund assets.

Then there's a marketing fee, called a *12b-1 fee* in Fundland. This covers promotional costs such as advertising and public relations.

Finally, there are management fees. Those are the fees that are paid out of fund assets to the investment adviser (or its affiliates) for managing the fund's portfolio. Basically, this goes to your manager's salary. So, sure, it makes sense that you have to pay the guy something; just make sure you're not covering his mortgage.

Do I sound cynical? That's because I am. I'm also lazy, which is why I like index funds. The fees are way cheaper and your returns will inevitably be better. Here's why.

The average actively managed stock mutual fund returns approximately 2 percent less per year to its shareholders than the stock market returns in general. That means that before your dollar even gets to the fund manager to invest, two cents has already been taken off the top. Now 2 percent might not sound like a lot, but over 50 years a $10,000 investment will compound to $1,170,000 at 10 percent returns per year, but to only $470,000 at 8 percent per year.

Nutty, isn't it?

These fees can really eat into your returns so don't discount them. There are a bunch of fee calculators on the Web that can help you determine how much of your returns will be eaten up by fees. Search for "mutual fund fee calculator" in your favorite Web browser—Google, for example. I like the NASD Mutual Fund Expense Analyzer (apps.nasd.com/Investor_Information/EA/1/ mfetf.aspx) because it's really easy to use. The Securities and Exchange Commission has a good mutual fund costs calculator (www.sec.gov/investor/tools/mfcc/holding-period.htm) as well.

To be fair, there are some fund managers whose services are worth paying for, because they are superior investors who are simultaneously fee-conscious. For instance, I just love fund manager Bob Olstein and have owned the Olstein All Cap Value Fund (OFALX) for years now.

So if you're not going the index route, which I highly recommend, you need to pick your funds very carefully. This brings us to the *prospectus*.

The Prospectus: The Key to Understanding Your Mutual Fund

A mutual fund is required to send a prospectus to its investors and anyone who requests it. It's basically a legal document/ booklet that details the fund's investment objective and policies. It also outlines the risks, expenses, and fees associated with investing in the fund.

Just about anyone will tell you to read a fund's prospectus very carefully before investing money in a mutual fund. But I'm telling you not to bother. The writing will put you to sleep and, let's face it, you don't even have time to read a box of cereal, let alone a 25-page tome. Besides, there are tons of journalists out there (yours truly included) who are paid to ferret out anything that seems fishy in a mutual fund's prospectus. Instead, do a Google search on your fund—or log on to Morningstar .com, my favorite mutual fund site.

Don't throw the prospectus away, however. There are a few specific sections you can flip to without much pain. First, read the Objectives and Policies section. It'll tell you how the fund plans to invest your money and what risks are involved in owning the fund.

Then find the fees table. This will give you a rundown of all the fees—including loads—that the fund will charge. Passively managed funds should have low expense ratios, from as low as 0.14 percent to 0.35 percent per year. Actively managed fund expense ratios tend to be much higher. They can go up to 2 percent per year for asset classes that are expensive to administer, such as emerging market equities.

Thanks to a recent governmental crackdown on fund families for slipping fees by investors, the prospectus is now required to show the effect of those expenses on a hypothetical $10,000 investment over 1-, 3-, 5-, and 10-year time periods. So flip right to the little chart and compare it to other funds.

Next, check the after-tax returns table. That's the money you take home after paying Uncle Sam. Again, this is shown on a hypothetical $10,000 investment so check it out.

Finally, check out how long your fund manager has been around. This is important for two reasons. First, we all like someone with experience at the helm. Second, with manager turnover comes portfolio turnover. The new manager tends to sell the holdings the last guy bought and start over with a clean slate. That may sound great, but it could mean a huge tax hit to you when he decides to sell everything.

If you're really crunched for time and have no interest in reading a prospectus—who does?—just go to Morningstar.com. Just enter in your fund's ticker symbol and all the important info will come up, including 1-, 3-, 5-, and 10-year returns; after-tax returns; and the fund's objective. Besides, conducting your research online lets you shop for shoes and learn about your mutual fund at the same time.

Mixing in Exchange-Traded Funds

Every season I take a day just to stroll the department stores. I'm talking about the good ones: Neiman Marcus, Saks, and Bloomingdale's. I dress up, put sunglasses on (to cut down on paparazzi sightings, of course), and stroll the elegant aisles of the rich and famous. I study the latest creations from Dolce & Gabbana, Roberto Cavalli, and Prada, some of my favorites. What are they showing? What should I be wearing this season? I take scrupulous mental notes.

Then I leave.

You didn't really think I could afford to buy anything, did you? A Dolce & Gabbana T-shirt costs more than my monthly car payment. Instead, I leave with a knowledge of what's hip, what's out, and what I just "have to have" this season.

Then I go to *Knockoffville.*

Would I love to buy the real McCoy? Oh, sure. But how can I justify a $2,000 handbag fully knowing my mortgage payment isn't far off. Roof over my kids' heads or a fabulous handbag? It's a no-brainer. (Or is it?—kidding!)

Instead I find stores that rip off my favorite designers and still allow me to pay my mortgage. I'm a big fan of Bebe, Guess?, and Express. They're not the most expensive stores in the mall, but they fit my budget brilliantly. I know that every time I walk in one of them, I will find something I like that attempts to mimic the brilliancy of D&G, Prada, and Armani.

That's probably why I love exchange-traded funds so much—they're just cheap knockoffs of the market.

The Giorgio Armani of Funds

An *exchange-traded fund* (ETF) is basically a shopping bag of stocks that represents an index such as the S&P 500 or Nasdaq. So it's similar to an index fund or mutual fund, but with a few big differences.

First, ETFs trade like a stock. They trade *intraday,* which means you can buy and sell an ETF at any time throughout the day. If the S&P 500 hits a peak at noon and you need money for your daughter's upcoming wedding, you can sell your ETF shares that mirror the S&P during your lunch break. With a mutual fund, you can buy and sell shares only at the end of the day when its *net asset value* (NAV) is calculated. That can be risky some days; gains you have at lunchtime could be long gone by the time the market closes.

The second big perk to these knockoffs is that they're cheaper than actively managed mutual funds. There are never any loads, and the median ETF expense ratio was just 0.36 percent in 2006 versus 1.07 percent in the mutual fund world. That's just an average. As we discussed in the last chapter, an actively managed fund can see an expense ratio go as high as 2 percent.

I'm by no means slamming mutual funds. I think they're fabulous and own a bunch of them. But before the advent of ETFs, the fund world had cornered the market on cheap, easy investing. Kind of like Sears and Kmart were the only places for cheap clothes when I was a kid. Thankfully, Target and H&M staked their claim in *Knockoffville* with the panache of the Paris runways.

Taking Inventory

The market was raging in the late 1990s, and just about every mutual fund was doing well. (But people were throwing darts at stock picks and making money back then, so that doesn't say much.) Mutual funds were an easy way for folks to invest in that rocketing market, and money poured in. Everyone's 401(k) was exploding and folks were mapping out their early retirement. No one was looking at the fund's fee structure because no one cared. Managers took advantage of this subtle ignorance and quietly started to raise their fees. If you looked at your fee structure back then, you were probably paying upwards of 2 percent per fund. That's nuts!

When the market's bubble burst and everything came crashing down, fund managers actually had to start working again. Many of them were unable to sustain their gains of the prior years. Investors came to the grim realization that the big trip around the world might not happen after all, and they started to get conservative. As people paid more attention to their statements, they quickly realized that they were paying a ton in extraneous fees.

Not to point fingers, but Putnam Investments was one of the biggest culprits. People were losing money hand over fist back in 2000 and 2002, yet, as an example, the Putnam New Opportunity Fund B shares were charging a 2 percent expense ratio. That's almost as bad as charging $300 for a knockoff pair of Prada shoes when the real McCoy is just a few dollars more!

The media had a field day with these rising management fees, and as a result the public started to understand the fees they were paying. Even better, the Securities and Exchange Commission (SEC), the U.S. government agency that's responsible for enforcing federal securities laws and regulating the securities industry/stock market, got involved and demanded more transparency in mutual fund reporting.

Fund investors looking for an alternative happened upon the exchange-traded fund, which was slowly gaining popularity. ETFs first hit the U.S. market back in 1993 when the American Stock Exchange launched the S&P Depository Receipts, Trust Series 1 (SPY), called SPDRs or *Spiders,* which was comprised of stocks that tracked the S&P 500. Arachnophobia aside, the Spiders slowly became a hit. It was no surprise that others followed during the bull market of the late 1990s.

In 1998, an ETF that tracked the Dow Jones Industrial Average (DIA)—dubbed *Diamonds*—was introduced. This was followed in 1999 by the Powershares QQQ Exchange-Traded Fund Trust (QQQQ), called *Cubes,* which tracked the Nasdaq 100. These were perfectly timed for the raging bull market and perfectly positioned for the crash of 2002, when investors needed salvation from those mean mutual fund fees.

Don't Let the Secret Out!

You know what happens when the word gets out on a good thing: People go and ruin it. It's like the secret getting out on your favorite place to shop. Once people start going, the store owners raise prices because the demand is there.

The same thing happened to the ETF world. People fell in love with Spiders and Diamonds, so the investment houses created tons of them to meet the demand.

There are approximately 500 ETFs out there at the time of this writing and more are sure to come. The problem is that these ETFs don't just follow major indexes anymore. Now you can get sector ETFs that focus on a particular industry. For example, the iShares Dow Jones U.S. Technology Index (IYW) focuses on technology and includes companies in the software, computer services, hardware, and equipment sectors. The Energy Select SPDR (XLE) holds companies from the oil, gas, energy equipment, and services industries. In the name of full disclosure, I own that in my IRA. You can even buy an ETF that focuses on a particular currency such as the CurrencyShares British Pound Sterling Trust (FXB) or the CurrencyShares Swiss Franc Trust (FXF).

Following is a list of the more popular ones:

- *SPDRs.* Under the SPDRs umbrella are a bunch of separate ETFs that divide various sectors of the S&P 500 stocks. If you want to get the technology exposure from the S&P 500, the Select Sector SPDR: Technology Select Sector SPDR Fund (XLK) will do the job. If you were looking to beef up the energy portion of your portfolio, the Select Sector SPDR: Energy Select Sector SPDR Fund (XLE) is a great way to go.
- *iShares.* The iShares is basically a different "brand" of ETFs. Just like Nike and Reebok both make sneakers, Barclay's Global Investors offers ETFs called the iShares, just like the SPDRs. In 2004, there were approximately 120 iShares ETFs trading on more than 10 different stock exchanges, including a ton of technology-oriented

ETFs that follow Goldman Sachs's technology indexes. These ETFs trade on the NYSE, whereas most other ETFs trade on the AMEX.

- *Vipers*. This stands for Vanguard Index Participation Receipts. Vipers are Vanguard's brand of ETFs and are structured as share classes of open-end funds. Vanguard also offers tons of ETFs for covering many different areas of the market including the financial, health care, and utilities sectors.

This is by no means an inclusive list. There are plenty of options in Knockoffville these days, and an increasing number of investors are seeking them out. As we discussed earlier, when something is in demand, it tends to bring out the greedy side of the suppliers. It's really no surprise, then, that the fees on some ETFs, especially the esoteric ones, have increased. Granted, we're not talking about huge increases; the median expense ratio for ETFs in 2004 was 0.28 percent. But the average expense ratio for ETFs launched since November 2006 has jumped to 0.67 percent, according to Morningstar. That's not going to prevent you from feeding your kids, but it's an increase nevertheless. And when you start to get more specific—like the China ETF—the usually low fee jumps to over 1 percent.

Warning: Cheap Fabric May Fall Apart

There is a certain type of reviewer who thrives on slamming anyone or anything that becomes popular, whether it be a fashion designer, a movie, a restaurant, and so on. Why are we such a pessimistic society? A question for another book, I suppose, but the critics are out in full force these days when it comes to ETFs. Why? Because ETFs are no longer a sure thing. To which I reply: Is anything?

ETFs that follow the broader market are still pretty safe bets because over the long haul the markets do go up. Sector ETFs are much more of a gamble because you're placing a bet that a particular sector is going to rocket—and everyone knows when you gamble, the house always wins. Putting all your money in an ETF that mirrors the financial sector, for instance, presumes the banking industry is always going to do well. And after the subprime mortgage debacle, we all know that's not true.

Critics have also warned that ETF companies' efforts to distinguish themselves with new products have led to offerings that are too narrowly focused for most small investors' purposes. According to research by State Street Corp.'s State Street Global Advisors unit in May 2007, more than half of the 500 ETFs it monitored fell into a sector or specialty category. With all these new offerings, the inexperienced, cry the naysayers, can be tempted to play tiny dangerous niches.

Still, buying a sector ETF can be a great, easy way to get that exposure in your portfolio. So if you're looking for technology exposure, buying the iShares Dow Jones U.S. Technology Index (IYW) is a quick way to get it, as opposed to analyzing and buying individual stocks. Of course, there is always the possibility that the tech sector could tank. But you knew that going in, so don't invest your entire portfolio in it. Use a small percentage that you'd be willing to part with if the sector comes crashing down. Sector bets are not sure things. Investing in the overall economy—that is, the Spiders and the Diamonds—are your safety plays.

Comparison Shopping

Here's how ETFs stack up against other investment options:

- Dividends are not reinvested into an exchange-traded fund like they are in mutual funds. Any dividends you receive from a stock in an ETF will most likely go into your money market account.
- Most ETFs typically hold less than 1 percent of their assets in cash while stock mutual funds typically have 3 percent to 5 percent of assets in cash, though it's not unusual for

mutual funds to hold up 20 percent in cash when the market's shaky.

- When you buy or sell an ETF, you'll pay your broker the same commission that you'd pay on any regular stock trade. So if you're planning on monthly investments into your ETF, make sure that additional commission outweighs the ETF's gains. Most likely it won't, and you'll be better off with a cheap index mutual fund that allows free automatic monthly investments.

ETFs can actually serve two purposes. They can be great for the folks who have a lump sum of money and want to park it in a cheap index-based fund and let it ride. They can also be great ways to get sector exposure without having to be an expert stock picker.

So shop in Knockoffville. Not because you want to be trendy, but because you want to be smart.

Wrap-Up

So what's the take-away here? Stick with simplicity.

While there are tons of new boutique-type beers out there these days, I'd take a cold Miller Lite in a bottle any day. The same rule applies to the fund world. You can find a lot of actively managed funds that claim they'll beat the market, but most won't. I'd pick a simple index fund with its low fees and strict correlation to the overall market. Or I'll mosey on over to Knockoffville and buy an ETF. Again, stick with the ones that cover the broader indexes and have very low fees.

In a perfect world, I'm drinking a cold Miller Lite on a hot summer day while wearing my fabulous new shoes from H&M. What could be better for me and my portfolio?

PART

II

LOOK UNDER THE HOOD

Navigating the Financial Statement

YOUR "JUST GET TO THE GOOD STUFF" GUIDE

Y ou remember CliffsNotes, don't you? Those black and yellow guides that summarize the books on your college lit class reading lists? Of course, they were created to *supplement* the reading material, not be a *substitute* for it. Yet most of us used these notes as a stand-in for the book at least once or twice (more if you majored in English). As adults with busy, complicated lives sometimes, we still need to cut a few corners. That's why we buy premade cupcakes and prelit Christmas trees.

Unfortunately, our busy lives require that the same corners need to be cut when it comes to the dreaded *financial statement analysis,* or *fundamental analysis.* But if you're going to invest in stocks, bonds, mutual funds, or anything market related, you should at least be familiar with a company's financial statements. Many market pundits argue that dissecting financial statements is the cornerstone of investing. While I agree, I just don't have the time. So using the Web and my previous life as an auditor, I'm going to show you some great ways to pick out the important stuff from the financial statements and learn efficiently.

A company's financial statement is basically a bunch of spreadsheets with a load of numbers that tells you how the company is doing moneywise. On it, you'll see things like revenue, expenses, assets, and liabilities. At first glance, these numbers may seem overwhelming, but have no fear. I'm here to help you navigate it all. I'll tell you what numbers to look at, and which ones to skip right over. I'm also going to help you perform your very own mini-audit of the company you're investigating (in Chapters 6 and 7). These techniques won't help you find fraudulence or uncover the next Enron, but they will give you a better understanding of what the company's doing and how it's making its money.

"But why bother?" you ask.

To get smart. Just by looking over a few select numbers, you'll be able to answer some important questions such as:

- Is the company's revenue growing?
- Can it repay its debts?
- After it pays all its debts, does it have any money left?
- Is it in a strong enough position to beat out its competitors in the future?

If you can answer those questions, you're on your way to making a more educated decision about whether or not the stock is worth a second look. And if nothing else, when you turn on the TV and hear a reporter like yours truly say that Microsoft reported a net profit of $14 billion, you'll know exactly what she's talking about.

Find the Financials (Hint: They're in the Annual Report)

The first thing you have to do is find your company's financials. They are located within the company's *annual report*. To access a company's annual report, you have a few options. You can go to the company's web site and pull up its annual report, or you can go to the Securities and Exchange Commission's site at www.sec.gov. The annual reports of all publicly traded companies are listed on its site under their technical name, the *10K*. For example, you can search for "Microsoft 10K" and the most recent filing will be available.

There are three main financial statements in an annual report: the balance sheet, income statement, and cash flow statement. That's where you'll find most of your numbers. There's a load of text in the annual report as well. Management's Discussion and Analysis (MD&A) is definitiely worth reading. It is a summation of the numbers and the company's outlook.

The sleuths in the audience will want to read the footnotes to the financial statements as well. Here you can dig up juicy nuggets on lawsuits, lease payments, and stock option grants, which are not reported in the actual statements. But for the overcommitted folks out there, like me, who get home from work at 8 P.M. and still need to make goody bags for the kids' class parties, if, at a minimum, you just read the MD&A and go over the cash flow statement, you'll have a decent idea of what's going on behind management's closed doors.

The main reason you need the full annual report is to read some of the text such as the MD&A, letter to the shareholders, and the footnotes, for the ambitious crowd. Otherwise, sites such as my favorites, Yahoo! Finance (finance.yahoo.com) or Google Finance (finance.google.com/finance), will have your company's financial statements there as part of your stock's profile. Just type in your company's ticker symbol and you'll find what you need.

One big thing to keep in mind during all this: These numbers make no sense when they stand alone. Granted, every company must prepare its financial statements the same way. All U.S. publicly traded companies have to follow a bunch of rules put together by the accountants, called the Generally Accepted Accounting Principles (GAAP), so there's consistency in the numbers from one company to another. But you still need to compare your company's performance to its industry peers so you can get a better feel for where it stands.

This is again where I turn to the Web to do all my comparison shopping. On Yahoo! Finance, click the Competitors link and your company will be compared to several peers and its overall industry. While Google Finance redirects you to Reuters with its Key Stats and Ratios link, you then can compare your company to its industry, sector, and the S&P 500. Either way, I just click away and don't even need to use my calculator.

The 10Q: The Reader's Digest Version of the 10K

The 10Q is a miniversion of the 10K, the annual report. It's basically a financial report that details what happened to a specific company over the last three months. Let's face it; a lot can happen in three months, so investors want to know what's been going on.

The 10Q is an unaudited document that the SEC requires public companies to file. It's a comprehensive report of the company's performance, due 35 days after each of the first three fiscal quarters. (There is no filing after the fourth quarter because that is when the 10K is filed.) In it, you'll find the balance sheet, income statement, and cash flow statement, a summary discussion from management, and some detail on the "material events" that may have occurred during the period such as stock splits or acquisitions.

Keep in mind that this document is *unaudited.* That means the company's auditors do not have to even look at it. Many auditors will review it to make sure there are no gross mistakes and many standup companies require them to do so, but the auditors do not have to offer an opinion like they do with the annual report.

Still, you can learn a lot about how your company has been performing over the last quarter in its 10Q.

Where to Begin

The best place to start when looking at a company's annual report is the MD&A. This big chunk of text comes right before the financial statement. We mentioned this back in Chapter 2 when you were ferreting out your company's dividend. That's because this is where management gets to tell you all the good things about its company.

The MD&A is a narrative introduction of the company's operating results and current outlook. The story may be enticing, but since the finance department generally writes this stuff, you can expect a lot of jargon and run-on sentences (no offense). Still, you will get a good overall explanation of the numbers here.

Before we begin, I should introduce you to the word *material*. Material is accountant/lawyer speak for any information big enough to affect the value of the stock price or influence an investor's decision. As an example, a $2 million expense is *not* material to Microsoft's $14 billion bottom line. Even if the company spent $2 million on a golf cart to get its founder Bill Gates from one end of the corporate campus to the other, it would hardly affect your investment decision since they're swimming in money, so it may not even be reported. (The press would have a field day with that though!) But a $2 million expense would be killer to a company like Verizon, which reported net income of only $6 million in 2007. So if something major happened, expect to see the word *material* pop up in the MD&A.

Now you can begin reading. You will find the company's financial results summarized as well as management's prediction of its current outlook. But anything out of the ordinary that has happened should be documented here as well. There may have been industry issues or a company catastrophe, so read carefully.

And be skeptical. A rainstorm might be catastrophic to a tobacco crop but if your company tries to blame a drop in sales at its retail store on excessive rainstorms, you have to wonder where everyone's umbrellas were.

You could be ambitious and go on to read the letter to the shareholders, usually penned by the company's CEO. This really gives you a sense of the company's personality. This letter will tell you more of what the company is doing and where it's going. Read between the lines. Are they moving in a direction that you're comfortable with? Maybe the CEO is announcing plans to streamline business and drop diversified areas. Are you happy with that?

Letter from the Auditor

The final thing you should read is the letter from the independent auditor, usually found in the annual report right before you get to the actual financial statements, though sometimes it's just in the back of the book.

Accountants write worse than attorneys, so you don't have to read the entire letter; just make sure it's issued by a major accounting firm like Ernst & Young, PricewaterhouseCoopers, or Deloitte & Touche. Then look at the last paragraph of the letter and make sure it says that the financials are "presented fairly." Some accounting firms may use the word *unqualified*, which means the same thing: all good.

If the letter says the accountants are giving a "qualified" opinion of the financial statements, that means they see big problems. If they say the company is a "going concern," run for the hills. That basically means keeping the business "going is a concern." So unless the company raises cash fast, it's "going" out of business.

Wrap-Up

This chapter has given you the background that you'll need to really dive into some numbers that we'll cover in the next two chapters. Reading the MD&A, the president's letter to the shareholders, and the letter from the independent auditors gives you a good sense of the character and direction of the company. So you're already armed now with knowledge. I love that.

Now, I said *some* numbers. Don't get nervous. But now might be a good time to refill your coffee cup.

CHAPTER 6

Auditing Your Potential Investment

Time to be an auditor. I know, you'd rather eat dirt. Me, too. I was an auditor for almost five years, so I know. But auditors are some of the smartest people out there—and for the sake of my auditor friends, I have to say they really *can* be fun. Indeed, we need these people. Think of auditors as numerical detectives looking for stuff that doesn't look right.

I'm typically a glass-half-full girl, but in this instance we have to put on our skeptic's hats to dissect the balance sheet and income statement in this chapter. Cash flow and earnings releases are covered in the next. You'll be happy to know that there's no need to break out the calculator. Use the Internet and my notes from the previous chapter and you'll be just fine.

Open the Company Checkbook: The Balance Sheet

Read a balance sheet lately? I know: far too many numbers to be enjoyable. Since this week's issue of *People* just arrived, you clearly have better reading material in your house right now. I would much rather read *People* myself, but I also know that you need to get familiar with this stuff if you're going to invest in the market.

This chapter isn't designed to teach you how to recreate a company's balance sheet. Companies pay accountants loads of money to do that, and the Web has excellent condensed versions. Instead, I'm going to show you exactly what to look at and what to skip.

Let's first talk about your personal checkbook.

To be honest, I don't balance my checkbook anymore. When I did, it was a complete exercise in futility because— being a former accountant—I attempted to balance it down to the penny. So when I was off, I was neurotic trying to figure out the discrepancy. Then I started banking online. The clouds parted and the sun came out. No more need to balance my checkbook—yippee! Of course, I'm still neurotic enough to check my bank account every day; but at least I'm not sitting there with my calculator crunching numbers. It's no wonder I can't get a date.

Still, as a woman who lives paycheck to paycheck some months, I need to know now exactly where I stand at the start of each day. The same holds true for a company's corporate balance sheet. It's a summary of a company's financial condition at a *specific point* in time. If the company's fiscal year mirrors the calendar year, at the end of the first quarter the balance sheet would be calculated as of March 31. The annual report's balance sheet would be compiled as of December 31.

The Purpose of the Balance Sheet

The balance sheet shows a company's assets, liabilities, and overall net worth. If you put it in the form of an equation:

$$\text{Assets} - \text{Liabilities} = \text{Net Worth}$$

Assets are things of value: the cash in the bank account, the employees in the office, the inventory in the warehouse, and so on. Those are obvious assets. Less obvious assets are a company's receivables. They're considered assets because that's the money owed to the company for the stuff it sold or the services it performed on credit. If the company has a 60-day policy, that means clients have to pay their bills within 60 days of receiving the products or they'll get hit with an additional late fee. While the company might not have the money during that 60-day period, it is *assumed* that the client is upstanding and will pay on time. So that money will show up eventually. That's why companies consider it an asset. It's cash that's coming.

On the flip side, a company has *liabilities*. That's basically the money it owes to people—kind of like all your monthly bills and credit cards. So if the company took out a loan to buy a new building, those mortgage payments are considered a debt liability. In addition, if the company bought items on credit, that bill is considered a liability.

A company's total assets less its total liabilities are its *net worth*. Think about your own net worth. Add up all your assets: your investment accounts, the equity in your home, the money in your pocket. Then subtract all the money you owe: your credit card debt, car loans, the money your parents lent you to buy your first home, and the like. What's left—if anything—is your net worth.

A company calculates it net worth—also called its *owner's equity* or its *shareholders' equity*—the same way. It's is an important determinant of the value of the company. As a shareholder, the last thing you want to see is that your company owes more than it takes in.

While you can learn a lot about a company from its balance sheet, remember that it's a picture of the financial state of the company at an exact moment in time. If the company bought a bunch of things on credit on the day it compiled its balance sheet, its debt account will be higher. Things would've looked prettier the day before it took on those liabilities.

The lesson here is that the balance sheet is not the end all, be all. Still, there are two important numbers that I want you to ferret out on your company's balance sheet: its book value (or net worth) per share and the debt-to-equity ratio. Granted, there are definitely more hot spots on the balance sheet, and for the super-motivated, we'll show you a few of those as well below.

But if you're short on time or anxious to get to your new issue of *People,* just find those first two numbers and be done.

For the People *Magazine Crowd*

Finding Your Company's Book Value per Share   A company's net worth is also called its *book value.* So a great way to get a cursory feel for a company's overall standing is to determine its *book value per share.* Book value basically tells you what the shareholders would receive if a company were liquidated.

You can crunch or click to get this number. If you're ambitious and want to crunch a few numbers, subtract the company's liabilities from its assets. Then divide that number by the number of shares outstanding and you've got the book value per share number. If you have zero interest in number-crunching (like yours truly), go back to your favorite stock site—book value per share should be calculated for you.

This fundamental measure may indicate that a stock is overvalued or undervalued. In very simple terms, if the book value is higher than the stock price, the stock might be undervalued and you just might have a buying opportunity. If the book value is less than the current stock price, it could mean the market has overvalued the stock and you should wait for it to settle before you dive in.

A word of caution: Compare this number to your company's peers before you jump the gun. As I mentioned earlier in this chapter, these numbers mean nothing in isolation. You have to compare them to a company in a similar industry to really understand how yours is doing.

Can Your Company Pay Its Bills?   Do your bills exceed your income?

Don't answer that. You might throw up.

But ask your company the same question before you invest in it. Excessive debt is clearly a concern. (Same goes for your big credit card bill.) So you need to determine how *leveraged* your company is. That basically means you want to know how much debt your company holds. If the company were sold today, could it pay off all its debt? A highly leveraged company probably could not.

As a shareholder, you're last in line for a payout if the company folds. That means all the creditors will get paid before you get the money you invested in the company back. So if the company can't afford to pay its bills, say goodbye to your investment.

The best way to figure that out is to check the total *debt-to-equity ratio*. You can run that calculation yourself. It's the company's total liabilities divided by its total net worth (total shareholders' equity). Both numbers are on the balance sheet.

A simpler option is to go to Yahoo! Finance or your favorite stock site and find it there. At Yahoo! Finance, drop in your company's ticker and click on the "key statistics" in the blue box on the left-hand side. Scroll down to the balance sheet section and the total debt/equity ratio is right there. If that ratio is under 1, the company probably has the money to pay its bills. If the ratio is greater than 1, you might have some problems.

A word of advice: Don't jump to conclusions. Compare your company's debt-to-equity ratio to its industry peers first. Some industries, such as the construction industry, carry more debt than others.

For the Overachievers

Now let's walk through some line items on the balance sheet where things could seem fishy.

Read the Fine Print   To truly dissect the balance sheet, you'll need to flip to the footnotes to the financial statements—that's the text that comes after the financial statements. The footnotes basically offer detailed explanations of any numbers that might not seem in line with previous quarters. If you come across a number that seems suspicious to you, odds are good there will be an explanation of the "fishiness" in the footnotes to the financials.

Pros love the footnotes. Many say it's the first place they go when reading a company's annual report because it's where all the juicy stuff is hidden. It's like "Page Six" of the *New York Post!* If you're looking for trouble—or trying to determine if your company is ailing—the footnotes are the place to do it. Management can choose to include only the good stuff in the MD&A, but the U.S. Securities and Exchange Commission (SEC) requires that the whole story be told in the footnotes.

Interview with Jim Rogers

Jim Rogers is hands-down one of the most insightful—and irreverent—commodities bulls in the market today. Although we also talk about commodities in Chapter 12, Jim's a stock analyst at heart.

He made his first fortune as George Soros's partner in the Quantum Fund and has been championing commodities to investors since at least 2004, when his book *Hot Commodities: How Anyone Can Invest Profitably in the World's Best Market* (Random House) laid out the case for a long-term bull market in hard assets.

I met Jim on the set of the Fox News Channel's *Cavuto on Business* weekend show, where we sat on the same panel every week for months. He has become a dear friend and I respect him immensely. So I picked his brain on what it takes to select good stocks.

> **Tracy:** How did you become a stock analyst and what do you love about it?
>
> **Jim:** I had a summer job in a research department on Wall Street. I knew nothing of Wall Street before I got there except that it was in New York somewhere and something bad had happened there in 1929. I did not even know there was a difference between a stock and a bond.
>
> I fell in love because my passion had always been to know as much about the world as possible and here was a place that would actually pay me to pursue my passion.

T: What's the single most important thing investors don't know about?
J: Balance sheets and the notes to the financial statements.
T: What's the most dangerous thing an investor can fail to realize?
J: The world is always changing. What is true today will not be true in 5 or 10 years.
T: What's the single most important method for getting rich?
J: Buying low and selling high.
T: Name the three investing information sources you use the most.
J: *Financial Times, Wall Street Journal, Barron's.*

Accounts Receivable   If you're enjoying your time with the balance sheet, then move on to the *accounts receivable* (A/R) number in the asset section. Remember, if a sale is made on credit, a corresponding receivable account will be created on the day of that sale. The accounts receivable balance is the total money owed to the company by the customer as a result of a sale.

If the company had a bad quarter (or year) and sales were down, you should've read about that in the MD&A. If that happened, the receivable account should be down, too.

If the accounts receivable are up, be skeptical. That could mean there are really old receivables still sitting on the company books that haven't been collected. Look for an explanation in the financial statement footnotes before you get nervous. There should be a clarification. Remember, receivables are an asset on the balance sheet, so they're a good thing. That's why companies are very hesitant to write them off. So maybe the company extended its payment terms; but maybe it's not writing off older receivables. If a customer bought an item on credit over six months ago and still hasn't paid for it, it may be time admit that the money just isn't coming.

On a more technical note, when a company writes off a receivable, it's basically throwing in the towel on the customer who owed it money. That means the company sold an item and didn't get paid for it—so money that was once considered an asset is no longer coming in and now becomes an expense. Expenses eat away at the bottom line—the company's *net income*—and lowering net income is clearly taboo on Wall Street.

A big A/R balance can also mean that the company is having problems collecting the money it's owed (perhaps they should call Tony Soprano). That's a management issue and you have a right to be concerned. Still, compare this number to its peers before you panic.

Inventory   The same logic you used to analyze the receivable accounts can be applied to the inventory account. Inventories are the items that are held for sale in the ordinary course of business but also include raw materials, factory supplies, and any items that are works-in-process.

If sales are up, that means the company sold a ton of merchandise. Inventory should therefore be pretty low. But if the number is still relatively high compared to last year's, something could be fishy. The company may be holding on to useless inventory and not writing off obsolete items. On the flip side, it could also mean that the company is coming out with a new product, so it's stocking up on raw materials.

An abnormally high inventory number may mean that the company is accumulating too much inventory before an actual sale is made. Either way, there may be very good reasons for this high balance. Reread the MD&A and check out the inventory footnote for an explanation.

While you're reading the footnotes, check out the accounting policy footnote, titled Summary of Accounting Policies. It's usually the first footnote in the section and look for any changes in inventory valuation. Most companies generally use *FIFO,* first in, first out. This means the first item manufactured is the first item sold. *LIFO* is another method. Here, it's last in, first out, so the item that was most recently produced is the first to be sold.

A switch in valuation methods is a flag. Many times, a switch happens for economic or tax reasons. It shouldn't happen very often. Be concerned if the company switches back and forth. Again, depending on the industry, inventory may be a nonissue. A service company will barely have any inventory on hand, whereas a toy company will have plenty.

Check the Company Report Card: The Income Statement

Now that you've reviewed the company checkbook (and hopefully liked what you saw), it's time to read the company report card: the *income statement.*

The income statement adds up all the company's revenues, subtracts its expenses, and gives you the bottom line— net income or profit. This is a big deal. You want to know that there's money left over after the expenses are covered because that's how the company can keep growing. No money left equals no future.

Formerly known as the *profit and loss statement* (P&L), the income statement helps you determine if your company is making money selling its products or services. In addition, it helps you evaluate past performance and potentially helps you predict its future. That's because it summarizes a company's revenue and expenses for a specific period of time, either the entire fiscal year or a quarter of it, depending on whether you're reading the annual 10K or quarterly 10Q.

Either way, it's pretty much like your child's report card. So dissecting the income statement can give you important insight into how the company did all year. Did it sell any products? Did it control its expenses? How much did it pay in taxes?

One of the biggest reasons many pros read the income statement is that it can tip you off to fraud. If management is overly "creative," you might be able to spot it here. Over the years, there have been two basic types of fraud:

- Fictitiously beefing up revenues
- Falsely decreasing expenses

Either fabrication increases the bottom line. Remember, that's the ultimate goal: to get the bottom line up high enough that Wall Street cheers and more investors want to buy the stock.

The good news is that I can show you how to detect these shenanigans on the income statement. So put on your detective cap because I'm going to walk you through the hot spots.

Where to Begin: Sales

The first thing to look for on the income statement is sales (revenues). It's the first number, so it should be easy to locate. Revenues are the total money the company collected for any goods sold and/or services performed. Every time your company sells a product, it records a sale. Think about that the next time you walk into Starbucks and buy a grande skim latte with two shots of sugar-free vanilla (which is sitting next to me as I type). That $4 is considered a sale, and will be added into the total revenue number.

Clearly, you want your company to have revenue. That means people are buying its product or service.

Next, look for fluctuations in that revenue number from this period to last. The accountants say you're looking for the "percent change" in periods. Here's the old-school percent change formula:

New value − Old value ÷ Old value × 100 = Percent change

So if your coffeehouse sold 1,500 lattes last year but sold 2,000 lattes this year, its sales increased by 33 percent,

$$(2000 - 1500/1500) \times 100 = 33\%$$

Odds are good that I bought most of them. Note to self: Cut back on the coffee.

Not surprisingly, there are calculators all over the Internet that can calculate percent change for you. Check out Percent-Change.com for one example.

Another option is to go to a favorite stock site such as Yahoo! Finance (finance.yahoo.com), which also calculates the percent change in revenue growth for you too. At Yahoo! Finance, enter your favorite ticker symbol and click on the Key Statistics link on the left side of the web page. The percent change in revenue growth is calculated for you. Then go to the "competitors" section and see how your company fared in the marketplace.

For example, Microsoft's quarterly, year-over-year revenue growth in September 2007 was 13.3 percent, whereas the industry average was 10.8 percent. Its competitor Google (GOOG) saw a 57.7 percent jump over the same period, whereas poor ol' IBM (IBM) had only an 8.8 percent increase. If the percent difference is bigger or smaller than you would like to see, go back to the MD&A and reread the revenue section. Management should have addressed it.

While visiting Yahoo! Finance (or any other favorite stock site), check out the *gross profit margin,* or *gross margin,* number. That ratio is just gross profit (sales less the cost of the goods sold) divided by total revenues. For a manufacturer, gross margin is a measure of a company's efficiency in turning raw materials into income. For a retailer, it measures their markup over wholesale. Be sure to compare that number to its peers.

To Catch a Thief

I mentioned earlier in this chapter that beefing up revenue is a favorite of crooked CEOs. This can be done a few ways. It can be blatant, that is, where the company just books fictitious sales. That's what Cendant (CD), the travel and rental car company, did back in December 2002. It just made up sales to pump up revenues and presumed no one would catch on.

A more subtle method would be to record sales too quickly. Here's how to spot this: Most companies consider an item a sale at the time of purchase. If I'm in Starbucks and I decide to buy one of those really overpriced, oversized coffee mugs, the company records the sale when I walk away with my mug.

But what if management decided that once that mug came off the production line, it was (in theory) sold? The logic is that once the good is produced, it's salable. If it's salable, it should be revenue. That's a pretty aggressive approach. Just because the company makes a pretty mug big enough for me to bathe my youngest child in doesn't necessarily mean I'm going to buy it.

To uncover this, flip to the footnotes to the financials in the back of the annual report again and reread the Summary of Accounting Policies. This time focus on the section called Revenue Recognition Policy. It details the company's thinking on when to record revenue and will help you understand at what point in the sales process the company considers the event to be a sale. While there are definitely industry standards, be concerned if the policy is too aggressive for your liking.

How Much Did You Spend?

Let's move on to the expenses section. Expenses on the income statement can be anything from depreciation to salaries and every company has them. Expenses are subtracted from total revenues, so they can easily bring a company's net income (bottom line) way down.

Every company incurs expenses. This includes operating expenses associated with running the business such as sales and marketing costs, research and development, and the overall general and administrative costs of keeping the doors open. Ideally, whether you're a company or a household, if you keep your expenses low, you'll be able to hold on to more of your money and, in turn, increase your bottom line. I really have to stop buying shoes.

Sounds simple, right? That's exactly why the second most popular fraud occurs in the expense section. Companies sometime get a bit creative (read: desperate) in their attempts to keep expenses down. An aggressive company may decide to classify an expense as a long-term investment, arguing that the company will continue to benefit from the expense they incurred over the next few years. Instead of taking a one-time charge, the company would elect to spread the charge out over a longer period of time. The bean counters call this *capitalizing* the cost.

Here's how it works: Imagine that a company bought a big box of 10,000 paper clips for $100; but they don't think they're going to use all those paper clips during this period. They think it will take them four periods to use them all up. So instead of saying that had a $100 expense this period, they will instead record an expense of $25 each quarter for the next four.

Now, let's say its net revenue number is $300. If it recorded that whole $100 paper clip expense, they'd knock their bottom line down to $200. If instead they only took a $25 hit, net profit stays higher at $275.

This is a farfetched example, but you see my point.

There are accounting rules that explain which expenses should be a one-time hit (like certain start-up costs) and which expenses can be capitalized over a longer period of time (clearly not paper clips). But, remember, taking an expense as a one-time hit can really bring net income way down. So some companies try to capitalize certain expenses over a longer period of time to help to ease the pain. Let's face it, though—it's cheating.

That's what AOL (TWX) tried to do back in the late 1990s. AOL claimed that various marketing charges and other indirect costs associated with new subscribers should be capitalized over a five-year period because that's how long the average subscriber stayed on as a member (so it claimed). Unfortunately for AOL, the regulators didn't agree with that logic. Those subscription costs *should* have been expensed as a one-time charge up front, so the company was forced to change its policy. No surprise, its bottom line disappeared into cyberspace.

Paying for Research

Research and development (R&D) costs sometimes fall into a gray area, too. R&D costs can range from nothing to billions of dollars depending upon the type of business you are analyzing.

Unlike many other costs (such as income taxes), management is almost entirely free to decide how this money should be spent.

How much should a company spend on R&D? It depends. In highly creative and fast-moving industries, the amount of money spent on the research and development budget can literally determine the future of the business. If a drug company stopped funding the development of new drugs, its future profitability would suffer. So it has no choice but to keep the money flowing to R&D.

Should it be expensed in the year incurred, or capitalized for a few years because it can be a big asset to the company? During the tech bubble, there was no real accounting guidance on this, so, no surprise, companies were taking liberties. Thankfully, the accounting bigwigs got smart and just made a blank decision: R&D must be expensed. Whether you were happy with the call or not, at least there's uniformity now. The decision makes sense; with technology changing so much these days, research done today is generally useless next year, so it should be today's expense.

Read the MD&A for the company's R&D policies and procedures to understand its approach.

Operating Income vs. Net Income: The Debate Continues

Once you subtract operating expenses from gross profit, you have your company's operating income. This number is strictly based on the operations of the business. And many will argue that this is the true bottom line of a company.

That's because some esoteric accounting expenses, like taxes, depreciation, and amortization and other nonrecurring charges, are then subtracted from operating income on the income statement to derive the final net income number. Many pros believe that these expenses have nothing to do with the company's actual performance. Those folks would just end the income statement at the operating income number and be done.

But regardless of their opinions, every public company must comply with the Generally Accepted Accounting Principles (GAAP), and the rules require that those expenses are subtracted from operating income to derive a final net income number. In the interest of consistency from one company to another, you should look at both numbers.

EBITDA (or Should I Say, Ebit-DUH)

Ebit-who?

EBITDA. We pronounced it EE-BIT-DAH in graduate school, though I've heard people say EHB-IT-DAH. Either way, it's such a useless metric that it's not even worth learning how to pronounce.

EBITDA is an acronym for *earnings before interest, tax, depreciation, and amortization.* It tells an investor how much money a company would have made if it didn't have to pay its loan interest or taxes, or take depreciation and amortization charges. To calculate EBITDA, take the net income number and subtract interest, tax, depreciation, and amortization costs.

In a nutshell, it's a number that was used a ton by Wall Street analysts back during the tech bubble when they couldn't find a company with real profits.

The argument *for* EBITDA is that interest, taxes, depreciation, and amortization are esoteric expenses. They don't really have anything to do with a company's day-to-day costs of running a business. That may be true, but you still have to pay for them! That's like my kids thinking if they don't see the chocolate pudding that they spilled on the floor, they shouldn't have to clean it up. But those expenses need to be paid, and the pudding better be cleaned up before I count to 10.

Think about it. If your company went to the bank to get a loan for the new plant it was building, the loan officer would most definitely want to know its tax and interest bills. So should you.

If you ever hear a company's management tout its EBITDA number, laugh to yourself because you get it. They clearly can't make money, so they're trying to dress up their failures by reporting an increase in *something* to investors.

What's So Extraordinary about That?

You should also be skeptical of nonrecurring costs and extraordinary items. These are some of the most abused areas of the income statement. That's because there's so much room for interpretation.

Theoretically, nonrecurring items are just that—things that don't happen often. Common nonrecurring costs come from discontinued operations. If a company closes a plant, costs such as selling unused assets or severance pay are incurred.

Extraordinary items are both unusual and infrequent. Frost damage in Canada would not qualify, but frost damage in the tropics would.

These expenses can be a tough sell. Expenses incurred from the devastating hurricanes in New Orleans in 2005 did not qualify (I swear!) because they are par for the course in that area. In actuality, there hasn't really been a truly extraordinary event in a long time. If the company you're reviewing shows extraordinary expenses, read the MD&A closely. Both extraordinary and nonrecurring items come *after* operating income on the income statement, so many companies will try to sneak stuff in so that it doesn't affect operating numbers.

Once those costs are subtracted, you'll finally arrive at net income—sometimes called earnings, profits, or the bottom line. This is truly what the company has left after subtracting all its expenses from its total revenue. Ideally, that number's not red. If it is, ask yourself why. Is it a start-up? Is it in dire straits?

Finally, look at the profit margin by clicking the Key Statistics link on Yahoo! Finance for your desired company. That's the percentage of sales the company has left over as profit after paying all its expenses. The profit margin tells you how much profit a company makes for every $1 it generates in revenue. Profit margins vary by industry, but all else being equal, the higher a company's profit margin compared to its competitors, the better. As with other line items, compare this number to industry peers.

What's Left

You'll also find dividends and *earnings per share* (EPS) on the income statement. You want to see that a company is giving a dividend back to its shareholders, and we talked about how to analyze a company that offers a dividend back in Chapter 2.

EPS is pretty much what's left for the shareholders when all is said and done. It's basically net earnings divided by all the outstanding shares. We'll talk about EPS more in Chapter 10, when I show you how use the price-to-earnings ratio to evaluate a stock.

Wrap-Up

How's your company doing so far? We've gone through the balance sheet and the income statement, so you should have a pretty decent idea of your company's financial health. What does your company's report card look like? Is it doing okay? Making money, I hope?

We've really only scratched the surface here, but this should give you an idea of what management is doing with your money when you invest in the company.

How's your head? Spinning, I'm sure. But you're learning— and that just means you're setting yourself up to make more money.

Cash Is the Real Deal.
Earnings Reports Are Not.

With two number-crunching documents down, the balance sheet and income statement, we have two to go—the cash flow statement and quarterly earnings release.

As trite as it sounds, cash is king. Reading the cash flow statement could be one of the most important things you do when analyzing your favorite stock.

Earnings releases, on the other hand, are not so dire. You should absolutely read them to get a feel for how your company did over the past quarter. But know this: They are not policed like the cash flow statement and the other financial statements. Management is free to say whatever it wants in an earnings release. If no one is forcing you to report bad news, would you?

Find Your Two Dollars on the Cash Flow Statement

"I want my two dollars!"

Remember that line from the movie *Better Off Dead* with John Cusack? The paperboy chased Cusack's character throughout most of the film because he wanted to get paid for his weekly newspaper deliveries, and Cusack never had the cash to pay him.

"Two dollars!"

Cracked me up.

As much as everyone thinks the world has gone totally plastic, you still need cash in your pocket. Because the paper carrier, along with the kids that sell lemonade on the street and your daughter who needs milk money for school, doesn't really care if you have a $1 million home and $500,000 in your 401(k). They (and you) need cash at all times to cover some daily expenses.

So do companies. A company with cash in its coffers is perceived to be a strong, well-run business. If you come across a company that doesn't have any cash, be critical. It *could* mean the company is expanding its operations and that's part of the overall growth strategy. If that's not noted somewhere, though—like in the MD&A—you might want to take your hard-earned money elsewhere.

The best way to determine if a company has any cash is to read its *cash flow statement*. That means we're back to the 10Q or annual report. The cash flow statement explains the company's overall cash position, so many will argue that it's the most important of the three statements. Yet, while it clearly offers a ton of information, the cash flow statement is not perfect.

The cash flow statement shows cash coming in and out of the business, but it doesn't show the stuff the company owes such as its liabilities. Think of your upcoming rent payment. Your checkbook doesn't actually report that bill until you pay it. But it doesn't mean you don't owe it all month long. Nor does the cash flow statement include the amount of future incoming and outgoing cash that has been recorded on credit. You'll find that on the balance sheet.

The same goes for previously purchased assets. They hit the cash flow statement in the period that they were purchased, so you'll see the cash leaving the company to pay for the new assets. But once they're paid for, those assets sit on the balance sheet. If you're looking at a company for the first time, the cash flow is not going to give you enough information about its asset accounts.

Regardless of these shortcomings, this statement is still invaluable. The days of investing in cashless companies are long gone and, quite frankly, just not smart. Back in the late 1990s, it didn't matter if a start-up company had any money at all, as long as it had a technology-related product. Back then, Wall Street analysts assumed any tech stock would rock. And they did for a time. Then tons of people lost their shirts when it was all over.

These days, your company better have money to pay the bills, expand its business, and issue you a dividend or you're out of there. Keep in mind that companies go bankrupt because they cannot pay their bills, not because they didn't report a good profit number. For that reason, many pros would argue that if you have to make a choice, the cash flow statement is the one you should read. Still, so many people don't read it or even know *how* to read it.

Don't be intimidated. As you'll see in the following sections, reading a cash flow statement is a piece of cake. The cash flow statement is divided into three parts—cash flow from operations, investing, and financing—and we'll go through each of them. An excerpt from Microsoft's cash flow statement is presented in Table 7.1

Net Cash Flow from Operations

We'll begin with the *net cash flow from operations* number, which is also known as the *total cash flow from operations* or *cash flow from operating activities* as it says in Microsoft's statement in Table 7.1. It's at the bottom of the first section and is probably the most important number on the statement. It tells you if the company can afford to run its day-to-day business. Net operating cash is basically all the money it collected from its paid sales (not the stuff still sitting in the accounts receivable account on the balance sheet that was purchased on credit) less the cash it needs to keep the front door open.

Table 7.1   Microsoft Cash Flow Statement

Period Ending	30-Jun-07	30-Jun-06	30-Jun-05
Net income	14,065,000	12,599,000	12,254,000
Operating Activities, Cash Flows Provided by or Used In			
Depreciation	1,440,000	903,000	855,000
Adjustments to net income	1,181,000	3,299,000	3,322,000
Changes in accounts receivables	(1,764,000)	(2,071,000)	(1,243,000)
Changes in liabilities	2,656,000	1,128,000	1,641,000
Changes in inventories	—	—	—
Changes in other operating activities	218,000	(1,454,000)	(224,000)
Total cash flow from operating activities	17,796,000	14,404,000	16,605,000
Investing Activities, Cash Flows Provided by or Used In			
Capital expenditures	(2,264,000)	(1,578,000)	(812,000)
Investments	9,503,000	10,230,000	16,046,000
Other cash flows from investing activities	(1,150,000)	(649,000)	(207,000)
Total cash flows from investing activities	6,089,000	8,003,000	15,027,000
Financing Activities, Cash Flows Provided by or Used In			
Dividends paid	(3,805,000)	(3,545,000)	(36,112,000)
Sale purchase of stock	(20,793,000)	(17,106,000)	(4,948,000)
Net borrowings	—	—	—
Other cash flows from financing activities	54,000	89,000	(18,000)
Total cash flows from financing activities	(24,544,000)	(20,562,000)	(41,078,000)
Effect of exchange rate changes	56,000	18,000	(7,000)
Change in cash and cash equivalents	($603,000)	$1,863,000	($9,453,000)

Source: Yahoo! Finance

Obviously, you're looking for a positive number, so if it's red, put on your skeptic's hat. But compare that number to the prior period before you panic. If you're looking at a quarterly report, compare it to last quarter. If it's the annual report, compare it to last year.

There's no real need to crunch any numbers yet, just eyeball it to get a sense of the trend. If you see some sort of steady or positive trend, take comfort that your company can probably afford itself. Be skeptical of big pops or one-time items such as a tax refund, which are also reported in this section. We know that you can't depend on getting a tax refund every year.

If net operating cash is negative or decreasing, dig harder. What's going on? Is it a start-up? Then the company may be using cash to get the business off the ground. If it's an established company, with decreasing operating cash, that could be a sign that sales are slumping or things are not being properly managed.

Before we dive into the next two sections of the cash flow sheet, scroll all the way down to the very bottom of the cash flow statement and look at the line titled "Net Change in Cash and Cash Equivalents." That's the change in total cash from the beginning of the period to the end of the period.

If you're feeling ambitious, flip to the balance sheet. The difference in the cash and cash equivalents section on the balance sheet from one period to the next should mirror the net change in cash and cash equivalents over the same periods. I'm just trying to pull it all together for you. Again, you'd like to see the net change in cash and cash equivalents increasing over the period. If the company's overall cash balance is down, then you'll need to read the next two sections to understand why.

Investing and Financing Sections

Cash flow from investing activities shows the cash coming in and out from income-producing assets. So if a company bought or sold a new business or division, you'd see the cash outflow or inflow here. Same goes for cash spent buying or selling equipment. In addition, if your company has an investment account that it uses to make a little extra dough with its unused money (in a money market account, for example), you'll see that gain or loss here, too.

Now move on to the cash flow from financing section. This shows the flow of cash between the folks it owes money: its shareholder and its creditors. Negative numbers are not unusual in this section because cash is coming out of the business, especially if the company is making its loan payments (good thing), buying back stock (another good thing), or issuing dividends (even better). Those are big cash outflows and are all reported here.

Be skeptical nevertheless. Flip to the debt footnote and understand what loans are coming due. Then be sure to read up on its dividend policy. Whenever cash is leaving your company, or your pocket, you should understand why.

Crooked Cash Flow

In the past, most accounting trickery could be found on the balance sheet and income statement as we discussed in the previous chapters—that is, reporting fictitious sales to boost revenues, letting old accounts receivables linger to keep the asset balance high, inflating expenses. But the accounting police have caught on to those scams, so managers had to figure out a new place to get creative. So they moved on to one of the least-read parts of the financials—the cash flow statement.

Until recently, only Wall Street analysts read the cash flow statement because the average investor just didn't understand it. (Not anymore!) Since so many professionals believe that net cash flow from operations is the most important number in all of the financial statements, it's no surprise that company managers wanted to pump up that number as much as they could.

That's what Pier One (PIR) tried to do back in 2005. It attempted to report a cash inflow in the cash from operations section that should've been reported in its investing section. So Pier One inflated is net cash flow from operations cash number. Since more investors are reading the cash flow statement and it's getting more publicity, the SEC thankfully caught on and insisted the company restate it. And while the net effect was zero, its revised net operating cash fell 64% in 2005 from $142.2 million to $51.1 million, according to the AccountingObserver.com, hands-down one of the best accounting blogs out there. Check it out at www.accountingobserver .com/blog/.

Similar cash flow shenanigans were going on at GM (GM), Popular (BPOP), Blockbuster (BBI), Vail Resorts (MTN), and BCSB Bankcorp (BCBS), according to the AccountingObserver. com. All attempted to beef up their net operating cash flow number for the sake of "appearance." Well, they have had to restate. And, no surprise, almost every restatement lowered their cash from operations number.

Why can't we just tell the truth?

But it's a good reminder that while the cash-from-operations figure is probably the single most viewed number on the cash flow statement, you still have to look at it with skepticism.

Earnings Release: The Ultimate Optimist

We said cash is the real McCoy. It's one of the most important numbers that you should look at when dissecting your company's financial health. Hone in on it and take a lack of cash seriously.

While you have to take the cash flow statement as well as other financial statements seriously, there is a document that your company puts out that you don't need to lose sleep over: its *quarterly earnings releases*. I'll tell you why.

The earnings release comes out four times a year, during a period aptly dubbed *earnings season*. During this time, companies traditionally report their quarterly or annual earnings results to investors and issue their earnings releases. Big warning: A lot of cheerleading goes on during this time.

"Hi folks. The quarter's over and we did just great! Here are the numbers to prove it."

That's how nearly every company attempts to present itself each quarter.

You'll know exactly when it's the quarterly earnings release season from the business news channels and web sites. The investing media will treat it like the Thanksgiving Day parade, reporting on it from every angle, 24/7 for the four to six weeks that it usually lasts. It's overkill, I agree, but it happens every quarter without fail.

You may find yourself getting caught up in it, eager to hear what your favorite company is going to say. (To find out when your company is reporting, I recommend the U.S. Earnings Calculator at Yahoo! Finance or www.earnings.com.) Take a step back from the hoopla, though, because earnings season can be a lot of smoke and mirrors—and I don't want you to fall for it.

Pretty Numbers Only, Please

I've always said that earnings season is a lot like putting an ugly person in a hot car. The initial presentation is dynamite, but once you open the door and see who's inside, you may be a tad disappointed.

That's because there's a lot of sugar coating during earnings season. Companies can opt to report only their sexiest numbers. Expect to see Lamborghinis and Lotuses leading the way. The ugly driver is in there somewhere, but he'll definitely be behind tinted windows.

Why aren't companies straight up with you during earnings season? Because earnings releases are not policed. While financial companies must include specific numbers and events in their financial statements, company auditors and the SEC are not required to review earnings releases before they go out to the public. There are no guidelines as to what should be included in an earnings release, so companies have the freedom to include only the most appealing numbers. Most of the larger companies will ask their auditors to review their press releases, but you won't see a note from the auditors saying they've reviewed it.

So if no one's really looking, companies have the ability to paint a very pretty picture. There's no need to mention the bad stuff if you don't have to, right?

Minding the GAAP in the Road

So does this mean the average investor should just ignore earnings releases altogether?

Hardly. There are still companies out there, such as Berkshire Hathaway and IBM, that tell the whole story. If you ignore your company's earnings release, you're essentially saying you can't trust management. If that's true, you shouldn't have the stock in your portfolio to begin with. The long-term investor, people like you and me, should just use these releases as information updates, fully understanding the motivation behind them.

So read the releases, but *be skeptical.* Watch for purposeful detours. If sales are down, but the company has two new products in the pipeline, don't be surprised if the release focuses on those two new products.

Be on the lookout for pro forma numbers versus GAAP numbers in the release. GAAP earnings are derived from the Generally Accepted Accounting Principles, the accounting rules that all companies are expected to follow when calculating their final earnings numbers. We discussed these rules in the previous two chapters. As a quick reminder, these rules often require companies to take big hits to their bottom line, which many companies argue aren't a true reflection of their day-to-day progress.

Since anything goes during earnings season, management can make the decision to just remove the numbers it doesn't think are important and come up with its own personal set of financials. These homemade numbers are called the *pro forma* (read: prettier) numbers. There are no rules in creating pro forma numbers. Anything that management regards as a one-time charge or irrelevant to the core operations will probably be excluded from the pro forma numbers. Don't expect to see restructuring charges, the amortization of certain intangible assets, or other noncash hits in the pro formas.

A stand-up company will hold your hand and explain to you the difference between the pro forma numbers and the GAAP numbers. There should be some sort of reconciliation somewhere in the earnings release explaining that difference. Go through it carefully and understand what management decided to call "unimportant."

Why must we do so much work to uncover the truth? What are they hiding? While it would be nice if every company just used the GAAP numbers for conformity's sake, until the SEC makes it a requirement, you can forget it.

For now, just hope that the numbers that make up the pro formas are the same quarter over quarter. At least then you're comparing apples to apples within the company. If the rules surrounding the pro forma numbers keep changing, it would be too confusing for investors.

Some Things to Look For

Earnings releases can be helpful if you're looking for a quick company update. In that case, what are you looking for? Increasing revenues, increasing operating cash flows, and new products coming down the pipeline. All that means the company is growing and selling product, which is good news.

Look at the earnings per share number. Did it beat, miss, or exceed Wall Street's expectations? That's the first thing the market will react to. Keep in mind that it doesn't mean Wall Street's number was right to begin with, but unfortunately that's the way it works.

New acquisitions should be discussed, as well as the segments it dumped. Make sure all this sounds satisfactory to you. Pay close attention to the company's "guidance." That's code for "Here's what we expect to happen in the future." If management is cautious or hints at a slowdown in growth, that will clearly affect the stock.

In the past, investors could look for some long-term guidance during earnings season, but it's becoming less prevalent. These days, if the company doesn't live up to its promise, disgruntled shareholders will proffer up a big lawsuit, so some companies decide that they're better off saying nothing. Regardless, pull out last quarter's earnings release and see if the company made promises for this quarter, and then check to see if they followed through. If not, are the reasons acceptable to you? Were there fundamental changes in the business that caused them to report negatively, which could mean more bad news, or did they just hit a bump in the road?

Finally, look for trends. When gas prices rose in 2007, many companies claimed energy costs were affecting the bottom line. Wal-Mart was among them, blaming gas prices for their financial problems. This is hard to fathom, as it wasn't like customers were driving cross-country to get to the stores. Wal-Mart just had internal issues that it was attempting to camouflage.

The same thing happened during the subprime mortgage blowup in 2007. Many companies blamed their bad sales on the ubiquitous problems in the mortgage markets, too. Granted, some companies did take it on the chin and were singing the subprime blues. Others were just again using the subprime mess as a scapegoat. So make sure the rationale is legit.

Get on the Phone

An earnings release is usually a single piece of paper, which isn't enough space to tell the whole quarterly story. If you're serious about learning about this company, it's really important that you listen in on the company's *conference call.*

A conference call is an actual live event where management talks to analysts and investors about the financial results of its recently completed quarter. Most public companies hold four conference calls (sometimes called *analyst calls*) per year, usually two to five weeks after the end of a quarter. Typically, the CEO or another top dog presents the company's numbers, followed by a Q&A session.

There are a bunch of perks to the conference call:

- There's plenty of time to talk about everything, including that GAAP versus pro forma stuff, and sometimes it's just easier to say something out loud than have the legal team attempt to articulate it on paper.

- You can listen to the tone of the executives and get a feel for how truthful they seem.
- The Q&A section allows analysts to put management in the proverbial hot seat. Granted, it's usually only analysts asking the questions, but you can eavesdrop. As with the tone, use your gut instinct. In the end, it's usually right.

In the past, the only way to listen in on a call was to actually dial in. Now you can watch most of these events on the Internet. Go to the company's web site to obtain a call-in number or to watch the live webcast. You'll learn more on that call than in any analyst's report.

Timing Is Everything

Most companies report their quarterly earnings before or after the opening of the markets. Reporting after hours used to be reserved for companies with bad news. The idea was to report at a time when not many people were looking. Two things happened that blew that theory out of the water:

- Investors started to assume that any after-hours announcement was going to be bad news, so regardless of the actual information, the company's stock took it on the chin.
- Pre- and postmarket trading became available, making it impossible to hide from the markets.

As a result, things have changed, and now, many traders say they actually prefer it when companies report after hours. Releasing earnings when the markets are closed gives investors time to digest the information. It allows them to think through the news—good, bad, or indifferent—and avoid rash decisions. It also puts everyone on more of a level playing field.

Reporting when the markets are closed doesn't necessarily prevent price spikes because of surprising news, but it does prevent knee-jerk reactions from buyers and sellers. This makes for more orderly trading, instead of the many meaningless gyrations that sometimes afflict stocks during earnings seasons.

Whether the news is good or bad, the stock price can really take a hit. These days, even coming out with a number the analysts were expecting, that is, meeting expectations, can cause the stock to move. For example, Google reported its quarterly earnings in early 2007. The company reported that its 2006 fourth-quarter profits tripled, but its net revenue was just slightly above analysts' expectations. Still above expectations, right? Should've been good news. Nope. The stock fell in after-hours trading because investors were hoping for a blowout.

So be aware. Earnings releases can cause big stock moves, regardless of what they say.

Wrap-Up

I would argue that the cash flow statement is the most important of the three financial statements. If you do nothing else, read that. To repeat, cash is king; you need it and so does your company. Be sure to:

- Look at net cash flow from operations number. Ideally, it's positive because that means the company can afford to run its day-to-day business.
- Check the net change in cash and cash equivalents. That tells you if the company has more cash on hand this period than it did last period. Again, you want to see increases.
- Always be skeptical. One number never tells the whole story.

Read these statements and hold your company accountable. If your company is cash-strapped, you might want to invest your hard-earned money elsewhere.

Put your skeptic's cap back on when those quarterly earnings releases come out. Remember, they're not policed, so many companies just opt to report the pretty numbers. A good earnings release should include numbers from the income statement, the cash flow statement, and the balance sheet. That means revenue, income, operating cash flow, receivables, and inventory should all be reported. Otherwise, you'll have to wait for the 10Q—the quarterly financial statements reported to the SEC—to become available to get the true meat of the story. That could mean your company may have something to hide.

Try to listen to the corresponding conference call. You get to be a voyeur and can really get a feel for management and its sincerity. Of course, you still need to be skeptical. So go through earnings season with the proverbial grain of salt.

We are officially done with the number-heavy financial statements. You survived your stint as an auditor and now you know how to ferret out the funny stuff. Congratulations!

Now on to being an economist.

CHAPTER 8

Breakfast with the Federal Reserve

GETTING THE ECONOMIC PORRIDGE "JUST RIGHT"

Parenting is one big balancing act. Juggling work, school, sports, play dates, and your own social life, what little there is of it, can be tough. Then there's that fine balance between being not too strict and not too lenient with your kids. On one hand, you want to let them dance on the kitchen chairs and just be kids. On the other hand, you need to enforce the rules, ensure they're well-behaved, and prevent them from becoming future criminals. Every night in bed, I torture myself by reviewing my daily decisions. Was I too hard on them? Do I need to discipline more? At this point, I usually get a headache and reach for the Tylenol.

Now imagine having to balance the entire economy. I'm not sure there's enough aspirin in the world, which is why I wouldn't give anything to be Ben Bernanke these days. Big Ben is the Chairman of the Board of Governors of the Federal Reserve System, in other words, the Fed. His job, to put it simply, is to make sure we have a "Goldilocks" economy—not too hot or not too cold.

Bernanke's balancing act is arguably one of the most important jobs in the nation and maybe the world. That's because Big Ben and his fellow board members at the Fed are in charge of keeping our country's finances in alignment. That basically means he has to make sure that the prices of the things we buy stay in line with our salaries and that there's enough money available to people so they can get loans, build buildings, and invest in the future.

The Fed manages this in a few different ways. First, it serves as the ultimate gatekeeper of the U.S. economy. Second, it is the central bank of the United States and all its member banks. And, finally, the Fed can stimulate or slow down the economy by adjusting interest rates or creating money (literally).

That's exactly why anytime the Fed speaks, the markets do cartwheels and the media pundits jump on the podium.

But what are they talking about, and why do they care so much? Let's go through the Fed's many different roles.

Where Did the Fed Come from and Why Do We Need It?

The Federal Reserve was originally created to control the money system in the United States. Back in the early 1900s, if you put that currency in the bank, there was no guarantee that you would actually get it back because the banks were not required to keep money on hand back then.

So the Fed was created in 1913 to help simplify the multiple currency issues and make sure you got your money back when you wanted to withdraw it. As time went on, the modern-day Fed, most recently led by the ubiquitous Alan Greenspan, became responsible for two bigger things: controlling inflation and preventing recession.

The chairman of the Federal Reserve serves a four-year term and is appointed by the president. He has a seven-member board of governors and 12 regional reserve banks beneath him. The president also appoints (and the Senate confirms) those seven governors. Once elected, they each serve for a 14-year term.

Ben Bernanke: Following a Giant

The current Federal Reserve chairman, Benjamin Shalom Bernanke, took over on February 1, 2006. As a former Fed governor, he was chairman of the U.S. President's Council of Economic Advisers. He completed his undergrad summa cum laude at Harvard University and his Ph.D. at MIT in 1979 (at the age of 26). He taught economics at Stanford and then Princeton University until 2002, leaving his academic work for public service.

Bernanke has stepped into pretty big shoes. Alan Greenspan ran the ship for the previous 18 years. Few had the power to make the markets move like Greenspan. When he spoke, he carried the weight of the Federal Reserve, forcing professional investors to analyze his every word.

While in office, Greenspan was often hard to understand. He reportedly once mocked himself during a 1988 speech when he said, "I guess I should warn you, if I turn out to be particularly clear, you've probably misunderstood what I said." Even retired from the Fed, Greenspan's words can still move the markets.

Inflation: Bad for the Porridge and the Economy

Certain things just shouldn't inflate—your head, your thighs, your credit card balance. Inflation is also bad for the economy because it slows economic growth.

Inflation basically means the prices of your favorite things are "inflating" faster than your paycheck. Let's walk through a very simple example from the television show *Sex and the City*. Carrie Bradshaw (played by Sarah Jessica Parker) wore Manolo Blahnik shoes daily, causing a huge increase in the demand for them. Every girl and her please-wear-stilettos boyfriend wanted a pair, so the amount of available shoes decreased. With the demand up and the supply down, the price of those shoes went up and up and up—but our shoe-lovin' girl's paycheck didn't.

That's designer shoe inflation.

Obviously, inflation affects more than just shoes. When the price of goods increases faster than the money we bring home, everything is affected. The cost of building homes, buying cars, and shopping for clothes increases. People consume less as a result, which can bring down a company's profits. With profits down, companies become hesitant to spend money because they need to preserve what cash they have to pay their bills. If they're afraid to spend money, they're certainly not going to expand the business or hire more people. This is what slows down the economy.

So with inflation high, things cost more and you spend less. That means you're not putting money into the economy to keep things moving, and that's bad. But when inflation is low—meaning prices are stable—consumers make more purchases and investments, so production output is maintained and employment remains high. So, ideally, we want to keep inflation low.

Recession: Bad for Your Hairline and the Economy

If the demand for goods falls—people aren't buying things—then the supply of those same goods could get too high. Production will have to decrease because there will be no need to keep making those products. If a company doesn't need to make as many products, then there will be no need to hire more people. So unemployment will increase. This can lead to an economic recession.

As an aside, unemployment jumped from 4.6 percent in January 2007 to 4.9 percent a year later, and many thought we were in a recession at that time. Now a person is considered "unemployed" if he or she is actually looking for work but is unable to find a job. The people who want to stay home don't count. So in January 2008, 4.9 percent of the people who wanted a job couldn't find one. (My advice is to look harder.)

Now, the official definition of a recession is when the total dollar amount of all goods and services produced—*gross domestic product,* or GDP—decreases for six months or more. I use the term *official* because it can *feel* like we're in a recession way before it officially starts. GDP may begin slowing down even though it's still positive. Again, this happened in 2007.

Other signs of a pending recession include decreasing housing prices, falling employment numbers, and limited business expansion. That makes GDP growth slow down and can lead to a recession.

By the end of 2007, GDP growth was clearly slowing. In the second quarter of 2007, GDP increased by 3.8 percent. By the fourth quarter, however, growth was only 1.3 percent, according to the Bureau of Economic Analysis (BEA). At that point, it was feeling like a recession even though, by definition, we may not have been in one.

There's an upside to a recession (I'm your glass-is-half-full girl, remember). It reduces inflation. The problem is that we generally don't want to go there in the first place.

As I already mentioned, markets can go down without entering a recession. We may enter a *bear market* without hitting a recession. A bear market is a just a period of time when the prices of securities are falling or are expected to fall. Although the philosophies vary, a drop of 15 to 20 percent or more in multiple indexes, such as the Dow or S&P 500, is considered the start of a bear market. That's kind of where we were at the end of 2007. And while people started to get nervous, remember something you learned camping: You don't fight a bear; you just wait patiently until it walks away, because it will. A bear market is a natural part of the business cycle. Markets go up and markets come down. Of course, I don't camp and haven't tried—but I've been told bears are supposed to walk away.

A *bull market* is a period of time when market prices are rising. Our most recent bull run started in 2002 and ended in March 2007. No surprise, bull markets are characterized by optimism, investor confidence, and the presumption that strong results will continue. And it's no surprise that no one wants the party to end. That's when you start to hear the term *bubble*—as in the Internet bubble of the late 1990s or the housing bubble of the early 2000s. Basically, folks get greedy and forget that what goes up must come down. Sooner or later the party has to end—the bears show up and prices come back down.

Of course, if I could tell you when that happens, I would not be sitting here at 11 P.M. trying to make a living while my kids are asleep. It's tough, if not impossible, to predict consistently when the trends in the market will change. That's called market timing, and only fools play that game. What makes it even more difficult is that psychological effects and speculation play a large (if not dominant) role in the markets. Positive sentiment could send the markets soaring, negative sentiment could tank them—otherwise known as a *market crash*.

This is where Ben Bernanke and the Federal Reserve come in. Thankfully, they have a few tricks up their sleeves to help keep the markets stable. Whether or not they actually work is fodder for another book.

How the Fed Keeps the Porridge "Just Right"

Remember, the fairytale about Goldilocks and the three bears? Well, apply it to inflation, which I know is riveting, but please work with me. The goal is to get our inflationary porridge just right, not too hot (high) and not too cold (low).

So how does the Fed do this, exactly? Through three big jobs:

1. It manages the nation's money.
2. It acts as the U.S. government's bank.
3. It acts as a bank's bank.

Job #1: Manage the Nation's Money

In its role as money manager, the Fed has to accomplish two things:

- Maintain stable prices and thereby control inflation.
- Ensure maximum employment and production output.

If it does those two things, we get a stable economy. To get things "just right," the Fed raises and lowers short-term interest rates. The pundits call this the Fed's "monetary policy," which is just a fancy way to say that the Fed can play around with short-term interest rates to influence the demand of goods and services. Here's how.

Let's say the Fed lowers short-term interest rates. That means it will become cheaper to borrow money. If you get a home equity loan, for example, it will have a lower rate. With a lower rate and the resulting lower monthly payments, you'd probably be more inclined to redo your kitchen this year. That, in turn, means that you'll be spending money on contractors, cabinets, appliances, and tile guys for your new backsplash. That helps the economy and stimulates growth. Lower interest rates therefore *can* be very good for the economy.

Of course, if interest rates are too low and too many people want to redo their kitchens, then the demand for new cabinets increases faster than the actual supply. Prices increase because of the shortage of products, and then inflation results.

See the porridge getting too hot?

On the flip side, if interest rates are too high, no one will take out a loan. Then there will be fewer people remodeling their kitchens, which means less money will be infused into the economy. Remember, if people don't have excess spending money, they're not out shopping for stuff and that means slow economic growth.

Now the porridge is way too cold.

Moving those interest rates doesn't affect just how we shop, it also affects who has a job. When the gurus refer to *maximum employment,* they don't necessarily expect everyone to be working. Believe it or not, it's actually healthy for the economy to have some people unemployed. I know, it sounds nutty. But if everyone is working, then everyone's getting a paycheck and that could mean that too much money will be infused into the economy again. Now you know that can lead to inflation and we just saw how that went. So economists generally like to see the unemployment rate hover just under 5 percent. They sometimes call that the *natural rate* of unemployment and playing around with interest rates can help them get there.

So now the Fed is helping to control employment, too.

Job #2: Be the Government's Bank

Another one of the Fed's big jobs is to be the checking account for the U.S. Treasury Department. The U.S. government does quite a bit of business and performs a lot of financial transactions. The Fed has to handle them all. These transactions amount to trillions of dollars and include every tax deposit and withdrawal for U.S. citizens. It also includes securities such as savings bonds, Treasury bills, notes, and bonds that are bought by and for the U.S. government.

The Fed is also in charge of distributing brand new money. Coin and paper currency is produced by the U.S. Treasury's Bureau of the Mint and Bureau of Engraving and Printing, respectively. The Fed gets to decide when it's time to throw new money into the system, and then Big Ben distributes the new money to the financial institutions so that they can circulate it into the system.

Pretty cool. But it is a balancing act. Sending too much money into the system can cause—you guessed it—inflation.

Job #3: Be Your Bank's Bank

Finally, the Fed acts as your bank's bank. Just as your local bank services its customers and offers loans, the Fed does the same for other banks. If a bank needs money, it can go to the Fed as the lender of last resort.

But borrowing from the Fed has a big stigma attached to it that basically tells the market the bank is in trouble and has nowhere else to turn for money. It's not unlike crawling to your father and asking him to help pay off your overblown credit card bills. What's worse for the banks is that the loan from the Fed must be reported to its shareholders. Then the market knows it needed cash and that is generally not a good sign for the company's future and its stock price.

Adjusting Interest Rates: The Long, Slow Simmer

Every time the news reports that the Fed adjusted the rates, streamers practically come out of the sky.

The Fed cut rates 50 basis points today!

But really, what's the big deal?

Here's what you need to know: The Fed did *not* cut the rate on your mortgage. If you have an adjustable rate loan, you *may* feel a little relief 6 to12 months down the road. But as far as you're concerned, your world remains status quo on the day of a Fed rate change announcement.

"So why all the hoopla?," you ask.

Changing the interest rates changes the economy, just not right now. It takes some time for that adjustment to work itself into the economy and make a difference.

But the media makes a huge deal out of it when the Fed changes rates, you may argue. Sure, because the Fed actually reacted to the market's current issues. The market was looking for attention like a little kid and got it. So the immediate effects of an interest rate change are psychological. It will be *months* before you actually feel that change in your wallet.

Let's walk through the three ways the Fed can adjust short-term interest rates. You'll soon realize why you can turn off the TV on the day the Fed announces a rate change and get back to doing homework with your kids. That has a much more immediate impact on your life than any change in interest rates.

What the Fed Is Really Adjusting: The Federal Funds Rate

When the media hounds (like yours truly) report that the Fed has cut or raised rates, it is referring to the *federal funds rate.* That's the interest rate that banks charge to lend other banks money overnight. Banks often borrow money from each other to cover their customers' demands from one day to the next.

Let's presume your neighborhood bank is short on cash. It can come to my neighborhood bank and ask for a loan at the going rate of, say, 4 percent. So your bank would owe my bank 4 percent on the loan. But let's say the Fed decides to lower that rate "50 basis points," which equates to one-half of a percent (see A Brief Tutorial on Basis Points). Now the lending rate is 3.5 percent. That lower rate makes it cheaper for your bank to borrow from mine.

That's a really good thing because if banks are willing to borrow more money from other banks, they'll have more money on hand to loan to you. That, in turn, infuses money back into the economy and stimulates growth.

A Brief Tutorial on Basis Points

A basis point is just one-hundredth of a percentage point (0.01%). That means:

25 basis points =	0.25%
50 basis points =	0.50%
75 basis points =	0.75%
100 basis points =	1.00%

So they really could say, "The Fed lowered rates by 0.5% today." But you might actually understand that, which would put a few pundits out of jobs.

The Fed's Bag of Tricks for Adjusting Rates

When the Fed adjusts rates, it doesn't just write the new interest rate up on the wall and say, "Voila! Here's your new rate!" Instead, it adjusts the available money supply to allow rates to move naturally, much like stepping back and letting your teenager make her own decisions. I'm not sure which is more stressful.

To do this, the Fed has a bag of tricks available:

- Open market operations
- Adjusting the discount rate
- Adjusting the reserve requirement

Once the Fed decides on a target interest rate, it then has to use one, some, or all of these tricks to make the market reach that target. The good news is that these tools generally work pretty well. The bad news is that we don't instantly feel the effects of these rate changes. It takes time to adjust the available money and notice a difference.

Let's dive into the Fed's toolbox and understand how it manipulates rates.

Open-Market Operations   The most effective tool the Fed has, and the one it uses most often, is called its *open-market operations.* That means it can buy and sell government securities—including Treasury bonds, notes, and bills—from its banks. There isn't really a physical "market" to speak of. This is just Fed lingo for the fact that it buys securities from the banks when it wants to increase the flow of money and sells securities when it wants to reduce the flow. This market is always "open" when the Fed wants to buy or sell something. Here's how it works.

Let's say the Fed wants to lower the federal funds rate. It decides to use open-market operations and purchases securities from a bank. It's the Fed, remember, so the bank has no choice but to sell whatever the Fed wants to buy. This is by no means charity work; the Fed pays for the securities, and does this by basically writing a check. The bank deposits the check in its reserve account and is required to keep a percentage of that check in its reserve. The upside is that it can lend the excess money to another bank.

So now there's more money in the banking system. That means it's much easier for one bank to get a loan from another so there's no need to charge extra or pay a premium to get it. That means interest rates between the banks, the federal funds rate, will automatically come down on its own. By now you know that more available money in the banks means more available money for you, which ultimately stimulates the economy.

When the Fed wants to tighten the money supply—or get the market to push that federal funds rate back up—it sells securities to those banks. The banks, again, have no choice but to buy them. Hey, the Federal Reserve tells you to do something, you do it. The banks buy securities from the Fed and pay for them out of their reserve account. Less money in the reserve, as you already know, means less money to loan to other banks. Money is then harder to come by, so the federal funds rate gets pushed up. This move ultimately slows down the economy by decreasing the amount of money banks have to loan. Less money around means interest rates go up and that typically reduces consumer and business spending.

By buying and selling securities to the banks, the Fed affected the entire market.

In January 2008, the federal funds rate hovered around three percent.

The Discount Rate Remember that earlier in this chapter I said the Fed also acted as the bank's bank. So when a bank gets desperate and needs money fast, it sometimes turns to the Fed for a short-term loan.

The Fed, however, doesn't lend money for free. The bank has to pay interest on its loan just like you and I do on our loans. The rate the Fed charges is called the *discount rate,* which is usually lower than the federal funds rate, though they're pretty close.

The Fed discourages banks from borrowing except for occasional, short-term emergency needs. But when times get tough and banks need money, changing that borrowing rate can affect our money supply. Higher discount rates make it harder for the banks to get quick money. Lower discount rates mean that the Fed is making it easier to get loans.

Now stay with me. With a *lower* discount rate, it's cheaper for a bank to get a loan so it will have more money on hand to loan to other banks. That means the federal funds rate will go down, and that was the Fed's ultimate goal in adjusting the discount rate to start with, right? You got it!

Many times the Fed will adjust this rate as a quick fix if the economy appears to be in trouble. That's what happened in August 2007 when the housing debacle sent the market into the toilet and everyone started to panic. The Fed lowered the discount rate from 6.25 percent to 5.75 percent (50 basis points) and let the market breathe a sigh of relief. It was a psychological move more than anything else; but it let the market know that the Fed was paying attention and calmed everyone down for the moment. It's not unlike your son's tugging on your pants until you focus on him.

The Fed had no choice but to continue to assuage fears and cut rates, thanks to the credit crunch and subprime mortgage fiasco. By the end of January 2008, the Fed had lowered the discount rate to 4 percent.

Setting Reserve Requirements Setting the reserve requirement is the third and final tool the Fed uses to adjust the federal funds rate and it's pretty straightforward. Basically, the Fed decides how much money banks must keep on hand at all times. The requirement is anywhere from 3 to 10 percent.

Let's assume it's 10 percent. Even though a bank has $10 billion in deposits from all of its customers, it only has to make $1 billion available. This ensures you that your bank always can give you your money when you ask for it. The upside is that your bank can lend out the rest of that deposited money ($9 billion) and thereby get more money out into the market. If the reserve requirement is raised, then banks have less money to loan. No surprise, this will have a restraining effect on the economy's money supply. If the reserve requirement is lowered, then banks have more money to loan.

Testing the Porridge

Now we know that the Fed can move interest rates, but how does it decide when it's the right time to pull the trigger?

Fortunately, Big Ben and his buddies have a ton of economic indicators to analyze and immediate access to all kinds of data and business contacts that provide valuable insight. By staying on top of where the economy is today and where it should be tomorrow, the Fed can (attempt to) project future changes and act accordingly.

So here are some—by no means all—of the economic indicators it uses in its decision process. These are some of the more common ones that you'll hear reported in the news:

Consumer Price Index (CPI). This shows the change in price for a fixed set of goods and services that are supposed to represent what someone like you and I might buy over a given period of time. It's compiled monthly by the U.S. Department of Labor's Bureau of Labor Statistics and helps the Fed measure inflation.

Real Gross Domestic Product (GDP). The GDP is the total of all of the goods produced in the United States, regardless of who owns them or the nationality of the producers. This number comes out quarterly and is used as an indicator of the performance and growth of the economy.

Housing Starts. Housing starts are an estimate of the number of housing units that started construction in a given period. It's produced monthly and is important because, as you know, home buys and sells are very sensitive to interest rates.

Nonfarm Payroll Employment. This number represents the total number of payroll jobs that are not in the farming business. It comes out monthly and it indicates the pace (or changes in the pace) of economic growth. The Fed can also get info on the total number, of hours worked and hourly wages, which helps Big Ben analyze trends in supply and demand.

Retail Sales. This is a monthly total of all merchandise sold by retail merchants in the United States. The numbers are adjusted for seasonality but not for inflation. It basically tells the Fed how much consumers are buying. It's sometimes called the *personal consumption expenditure* and it indicates future growth or lags in the economy.

Lightweight Vehicle Sales. Changes in car sales account for a large portion of the change in the GDP from quarter to quarter, so the Fed has to looks at this number, too.

Yield on 10-year Treasury Bond. This is just the current market rate for U.S. Treasury bonds that will be maturing in 10 years. But since mortgage rates tend to follow it, the Fed watches it closely. Changes in mortgage rates could obviously affect the future housing industry, so it's important to stay on top of that.

By keeping these economic indicators on its radar screen, the Fed can monitor the economy and foresee future changes.

Wrap-Up

The Fed's biggest responsibility is to keep inflation low and recession away. The Federal Reserve and its chairman, Ben Bernanke, spend their days trying to keep the economy from running too hot or too cold. It does this mostly by adjusting interest rates. If rates are too low, there could be too much money in the system, which could lead to inflation. If rates are too high, people may not be spending enough money, which could stifle economic growth. That could lead to a recession.

When you hear the financial news report that the Fed cut or hiked interest rates, you now know they're referring to the federal funds rate. That's the rate that banks charge each other to borrow money. Remember, it's like this: Federal funds = Friend-to-friend.

But to move that federal funds rate, the Fed uses a few different methods such as adjusting the discount rate. That's the rate the Fed charges banks to borrow money. That's like this: Discount rate = Borrowing from Dad.

And the Fed's ultimate goal? To get Goldilocks a good interest rate on her home equity loan so she can work on remodeling her kitchen and make her own porridge.

PART III

DECISIONS, DECISIONS

9

Will You Still Love Me Tomorrow?

GROWTH, VALUE, AND MOMENTUM STOCKS

We've covered all the macro stuff. You now understand how to read a set of financial statements and you've got a solid, big-picture economic background. It's time to hone in on things a bit and focus on analyzing individual stocks. It's now time to tackle these questions:

- How do you spot a good stock?
- Are the expensive ones necessarily the best?
- How do you figure out its growth potential?

The rest of the book focuses on helping you make some smart stock-picking choices. We'll begin with an overview of the differences between a growth stock, a value stock, and a momentum stock and how each of them could have a place in your portfolio. In the chapters that follow, we further analyze each stock by looking at its growth rate, its price-to-book ratio, and other well-known metrics that help you make intelligent investment decisions.

Keep in mind, there are a multitude of variables used to analyze a stock. So we're going to go over only the big, important ones here. The more you get comfortable with stock jargon, the more metrics you'll be able to incorporate into your analysis. Be patient. A lot of this will first seem like the Pig Latin you learned in the third grade. It sounds goofy at first, but once you get it, you can't stop using it.

Etslay etgay artedstay! (Translation: Let's get started!)

Growth Stocks: Hidden Gems

The Terminator is considered one of the most influential action and science fiction films of all time. The 1984 film, directed by James Cameron and starring Arnold Schwarzenegger and Linda Hamilton, introduces the concept of a "terminator," a seemingly unstoppable cyborg assassin who has been sent back from the year 2029 by Skynet, a super computer with artificial intelligence bent on the extermination of humankind. The terminator's mission is to kill Sarah Connor (Linda Hamilton), whose future son founds a resistance movement against the computer and its robot army.

The movie made box office history back in 1984 when it grossed $4 million during its opening first weekend. All told, the movie has made $78 million worldwide on a shoestring budget of $6.4 million. As Arnold Schwarzenegger's physique grew, so did his popularity. As a result, he received more money to revive his cyborg assassin character in 1991's *Terminator 2: Judgment Day* and *Terminator 3: Rise of the Machines.*

Think of Arnold as a *growth stock.* Shares in a company whose earnings are expected to grow at an above-average rate relative to the market are considered growth stock shares.

Growth stocks were back in vogue during 2006 and 2007. Research in Motion (RIMM), Google (GOOG), Amazon (AMZN), and Apple (AAPL) were good examples of technology growth stocks back then.

What Makes Arnold the Terminator

With growth stocks, you're basically looking for a stock that has a high percentage of growth in sales and revenue from one period to the next, compared to the rest of the market. This doesn't come cheap. Wall Street generally places high valuations on these stocks, so you pay a premium.

These companies may not issue dividends. They prefer to reinvest any extra cash back into the business than to distribute to shareholders. This means that you're in a growth stock for its capital appreciation, not income distribution.

When selecting a growth stock, don't place a bet on a company that's growing so fast it can't sustain the pace. Remember, companies that can grow earnings and revenues consistently are considered growth stocks. Companies like Walgreen's, General Mills, and Hershey's are generally going to sell more product every year, and are considered good growth stocks.

Historically, growth stocks have been in the technology, retail, and media sectors—but things change. In the 1990s, you would never have called US Steel (X), or any energy stock, a growth stock. Today, US Steel and energy stocks are considered solid growth stocks because they've been able to sustain a respectable level of growth over the last few years. US Steel, for instance, is up 777 percent over the last five years. That's damn respectable.

Part of the reason for the new growth craze is that a few stocks went nuts recently. Baidu (BIDU), First Solar (FSLR), and Apple have been flexing some serious muscle. Even though their prices went up, investors still like them and keep buying.

We're also seeing a changing of the guard. The old regime of growth stocks were companies like Electronic Arts (ERTS), Yahoo! (YHOO), eBay (EBAY), and Dell (DELL) were the stocks to own. These days, Baidu, First Solar, and RIMM are the new statesmen. So if you want to hold growth stocks, consider those in your portfolio.

So how do you find a good growth stock?

Finding Arnold

To unearth growth stocks, you'll need to crunch a few numbers. The first (and easiest) thing to do is to find the percent change in revenue from one quarter to the next. Go to Yahoo! Finance (finance.yahoo.com)—or your favorite stock site—and pull up the stock's summary page. Click the Competitors link and compare its quarterly revenue growth change to its peers.

Take Research in Motion. Its quarterly revenue growth in third quarter 2007 was 76.5 percent, while its peers Microsoft (MSFT), Motorola MOT, and Nokia (NOK) had growth of 32 percent, −1.8 percent, and 3.7 percent, respectively. Comparing Research in Motion's revenue growth to its peers reveals that it was a growth stock—the Schwarzenegger of the group at the time, if you will.

Do the same exercise for the bottom line or net income. You want to see big percent changes from one quarter to the next.

Then analyze the nonfinancial "stuff." You need to understand your stock's industry and trends, which is actually much harder than crunching numbers. Start with the company's financial statement, specifically the Management's Discussion and Analysis (MD&A, already covered in Chapter 5). This text in the front of your annual report is management's opportunity to tell you about the trends in its industry and how it's playing them. Have shipments increased? Are they selling more product than last period? What are the plans for the future?

What you're looking for are competitive advantages. A good growth company has a proprietary product that no one else has such as a drug patent in the case of Amgen (AMGN) or high-tech product in the case of Research in Motion. A dominant brand can be a competitive advantage—soft drinks and chocolate for Coca-Cola (KO) and Hershey's (HSY), respectively.

No one knows how long a growth stock phase will last because it's always a question of whether so-called growth companies can keep their annual returns up. If a stock stops its Terminator growth, what happens to it? It becomes either a "value" play or a "momentum" trade.

Value Stocks: Till Death Do Us Part

You will often hear the pros mention that some stocks are *value plays* and others are *momentum plays*. In a nutshell: The big differences between value stocks and momentum plays are in the creation and length of the relationship.

Momentum investing is similar to a one-night stand: You may barely know the person's name before you get involved, and it's usually over quickly. *Value investing* is more of a long-term commitment or a marriage. You take time to pick the right partner. Ideally, you meet when you're young and stay for the long haul.

Value investors such as Warren Buffett generally pick stocks that are out of favor or underpriced. This type of investor thinks the stock price is lower than it should be and believes it's only a matter of time before the masses catch on and drive up the price. A typical value investor does a ton of homework. She reads the financials and does some serious fundamental analysis (similar to what we did in Chapter 6 and 7), and typically looks for stocks with a low price-to-earnings ratio or price-to-book ratio. Once the value investor finds something she likes, she will buy it and wait, assuming that the market will eventually realize it's a good company and the stock price will rise. Then value investors will gloat because they bought the stock at a very low price, when no one was looking.

This slow and steady approach is exactly why value investing is generally recommended for long-term investors. It should come as no surprise that many value investors will argue that, over the long haul, value stocks outperform the market over the years.

Contrary to growth stocks, value stocks trade at a lower price relative to their fundamentals (dividends, earnings, sales, and so on), which is what many stocks were doing at by the end of 2007. That means the stock is undervalued and a good buy. These days, many would call stocks such as Citibank (C) and Home Depot (HD) value plays. Their stocks have been crushed because of the recent economic environment, but the value guys still see big potential in both companies. So value investing was making a comeback in early 2008.

Momentum Stocks: One Night Stands

A momentum trader does not buy a stock for the long haul. He often doesn't care what a stock looks like, whether or not it pays a dividend, or what its plans for the future are. He just cares that it's moving quickly—up or down, it doesn't matter.

One of my sources once said that a momentum stock is "simply a horse you want to ride for short time, and how quickly you jump on and off will determine your gains."

You can't be greedy in this game. You need to set a breakpoint and tell yourself something like this: "When the stock price hits X, I'm selling, regardless of how much more I think I can squeeze out of it." Then you get out while it's still good. This is *not* a buy-and-hold strategy. Momentum investors typically hold a stock for a few days—but it could be as short as a few hours—so they need to monitor their holdings daily. As a result, momentum trading can be very risky and requires a lot of time.

To find a good momentum play, traders look for a few basic things in a stock: a strong price chart, rapid earnings growth, and recent positive changes in earnings-growth forecasts. They don't spend a ton of time analyzing financial statements, but they do follow the trend. If people are talking about it, momentum traders are interested.

When Jim Cramer, host of CNBC's *Mad Money*, mentions a stock on his show, it sometimes turns into a momentum play. Here's how it happens: People watch *Mad Money*. They go to the office the next day and rehash the show with their friends. Then they all run back to their computers and start buying (or selling, if appropriate) in between meetings.

Another way to find good momentum plays is to use a *stock screen filter*, which is basically a computer-generated program that spits out stocks that meet a particular criterion. You can program a stock screen filter to find the stocks that have had the biggest percentage gains or losses over a certain period of time, or to list the stocks that have a really high volume. TC2000, MetaStock, and Genesis are examples of stock screen filters.

These days, you're sure to find pretty much any petroleum stock since oil prices are bouncing around—Halliburton (HAL) is a great example. The same is true of the Chicago Mercantile Exchange (CME), which operates as a futures exchange in the frenzied commodities world.

Each momentum trader has her own set of rules and parameters, but the essence is the same: Get in and out quickly, and take advantage of speculation. If you're going to play this game with the professionals, stay on top of it. If you don't pay attention, you don't stand a chance.

Wrap-Up

You now know the difference between growth, value, and momentum stocks.

- *Growth stocks* are stocks on steroids. They have big potential and everyone knows it so they're not necessarily cheap stocks. Growth stocks may not pay a dividend because they opt to invest any extra money back into the business.
- A *value stock* is one that you believe is cheap and has a good long-term potential.
- A *momentum stock* is like a one-night stand. You have no attachment to it except for the fact that it's moving, either up or down, and you can make money trading it right now.

Your investment philosophy and time horizon will determine which stocks you choose to hold in your portfolio. Once you decide on the type of stock you want to investigate, and there could be some from for all three in your portfolio, it's time to dig deeper into the individual names and decide which ones meet your standards. We do this in the next chapter.

CHAPTER 10

Evaluating Cars and Stocks

Shopping for stocks is a lot like shopping for cars. What you're in the market for will influence how you evaluate your options.

Let's say you're looking for a Lamborghini Murciélago or a Ferrari F430. Isn't everyone? You're clearly most interested in the superb transmission, the massive gripping, and how your date is going to react when you pull up in it.

If you're in the market for a minivan, on the other hand, you're probably much more concerned about the airbags, its capacity to seat your kid's entire flag football team, and the key fob's ability to open and close the trunk while your arms are full of groceries.

Picking stocks is fairly similar. Certain stocks meet certain needs for your portfolio, and there are many valuation metrics out there to help you make the right choices. While you should consider all of them, some metrics just hold more relevance in certain industries, and everyone has his or her own personal limits or cutoffs.

Price-to-Earnings Ratio

Whether you drive the Murciélago or a Honda Odyssey, certain metrics are evaluated with every car purchase. Take

127

miles per hour. Does the car do 120 mph or 180 mph? Clearly an important factor and one everyone uses.

The same goes for the *price-to-earnings* (P/E) ratio in the stock world. Many traders argue that it's the simplest way to measure how expensive a company is. If you're going to use just one metric, P/E is probably the one to go with.

Calculating the P/E Ratio

To calculate the P/E ratio, divide your company's current stock price by its *earnings per share* (EPS). For example, if your company's EPS is $2 and the stock is selling for $20 per share, the P/E ratio is $10 ($20 divided by $2). You can find a cheat that does this for you at Yahoo! Finance.

Most of the time, P/E is calculated using EPS from the last four quarters, which is why you'll hear it referred to as the *trailing P/E*. It's based on the historical data that trails behind.

Some analysts argue that a trailing P/E is not necessarily a good indication of the future. Others, such as Jim Cramer, use an *estimated P/E* based on the company's current fiscal year as opposed to last year's trailing numbers. It's much better and probably as close to a current P/E as you're going to get without calling up the company CFO and asking for the most recent P/E.

Still other traders like to look at a *projected P/E,* which is then based on future earnings. This is mostly based on guesswork and like looking into a crystal ball, so read those numbers with trepidation.

Don't Look at P/E in a Vacuum

The P/E ratio is basically the price an investor is willing to pay for $1 of the company's earnings. If the P/E is $10, it means that investors are willing to pay $10 for every $1 of earnings that the company generates.

But that means nothing if you don't compare that number to your company's peers. Each industry has its own "normal"

P/E range. For example, in October 2007, Internet search engine providers Google and Yahoo! had an industry average P/E of about $42, while the financial stocks' average P/E hovered around $12. (As an aside, those Internet stocks' P/Es were closer to $100 back in the late 1990s tech bubble.) That means people were willing to pay more for Internet stocks because they were still expecting big growth. The health care sector has always had a similar cache: Earnings grow more consistent so people are willing to pay more.

On the flip side, financial stocks such as Citibank (C), JPMorgan Chase (JPM), and Bank of America (BAC) are on the slow-and-steady path and had P/Es of around $8 or $9 at the end of 2007. Since they are less exciting, people aren't willing to pay as much, especially given that they blew up during the subprime mess of 2007.

Note that a company with a high P/E ratio, meaning high growth expectations, eventually has to live up to the hype. Take Microsoft, for example. Back in 1999, its P/E hovered around $75. That's because people expected the company to rocket, which it did. As its hot-new-company momentum shifted to boring blue-chip stability, its P/E dropped to $21. Nothing wrong with boring, however. Boring pays the bills.

Put a Peg on It

The best way to make use of the P/E ratio is to consider it in tandem with the company's growth rate. Enter the *price/ earnings-to-growth* (PEG) ratio.

The PEG ratio is just the P/E ratio divided by the company's annual earnings growth rate. It's a much better indicator because it looks forward and accounts for the company's future growth potential. Yahoo! Finance does the PEG ratio for you, too.

The basic rule of thumb is if the PEG is below $1, the stock is underpriced. If the PEG is greater than $1, the stock is overpriced. If a growth company's PEG is $1, the company is pretty fairly valued. Let's look at Goldman Sachs (GS). In December

2007, its PEG was around $0.65 and its P/E was $8.65 versus the industry's $17. No wonder many call the stock "best of breed."

The P/E ratio can be useful when trying to determine the value of a stock. It can certainly tell you a lot about a company if you use earnings growth rates in your analyses and then compare the ratio to other stocks in the same industry. But don't let the P/E ratio make or break your decision. Make sure you understand your company's fundamentals as well as the current market environment.

Price-to-Book Ratio

Next, consider evaluating your company's book value. The ubiquitous Jim Cramer has said that he wouldn't buy certain companies that were trading at more than two times book value.

In the simplest terms, the book value of a company is its assets minus its liabilities, which means it's synonymous with shareholder's equity (assets minus liabilities equal shareholder's equity or net worth). However, many money managers would argue that's not entirely accurate, and we touched on this in Chapter 6.

As a refresher, true book value does not include *intangible assets,* such as goodwill and other nonconcrete assets; those are strictly esoteric accounting items. To accurately calculate book value, subtract all intangible assets from total assets. What you're left with is the stuff you can touch such as the buildings, computers, telephones, and office chairs. For this reason, book value is sometimes also called *net tangible assets.* It's basically what's left if the company were liquidated today.

Keep in mind, though, that book value often reflects what an asset was worth when it was purchased, not the current market value.

Ideally, you should figure out a company's book value. Realistically, you're probably going to click over to Yahoo! Finance or your favorite stock site and put in the company's ticker. In Yahoo! Finance, click the Key Statistics and scroll down to Book Value per Share under the Balance Sheet heading.

Here it's nicely calculated for you. If the book value is higher than the stock price, the stock might be undervalued and you just might have a buying opportunity, but before you jump the gun, scroll up to the Price-to-Book Ratio in the same section.

What It Means

The *price-to-book ratio* measures what the market is willing to pay for your company's book value. A low price-to-book value could mean the stock is a bargain. A higher price-to-book could mean the market is putting a premium on your stock. It's willing to pay more because of future growth potential.

While the ratio is already calculated for you, you should understand what goes into it. First, divide the company's book value by the number of shares outstanding. That's your denominator. The current stock price is your numerator. So just divide the two numbers. Here's an advanced math lesson: If you hadn't already calculated book value, you can *back* into it using the price-to-book ratio. As a simple example, if the price-to-book ratio is 2 and the stock is trading at $30, that would mean the book value per share is $15 (30/15 = 2).

Similar to the book value calculation, the price-to-book ratio is most accurate with companies that have hard assets, like factories or equipment. That's why it's a good measure for banks and insurance companies that have a lot of financial assets because they either have the cash or they don't. In these sectors, you'd like to see a lower price-to-book ratio.

But just like the number of cup holders is completely irrelevant when looking at the Murciélago (clearly important in the minivan, though), price-to-book isn't a deal breaker in other industries. For companies that rely heavily on intellectual assets such as patents, trademarks, even their employees' brains, this stuff just doesn't show up on the balance sheet. Those companies indirectly end up with low book values because their most important assets aren't reported. Low book value generally translates into an inaccurately high price-to-book ratio—which is why you can't rely on this measure in all industries.

Every Car Needs Good Brakes

Regardless of industry, you still should look at the price-to-book ratio because it will give you a good feel for how your stock is trading against the rest of the market. It's also a pretty stable number over time since you're working with hard assets. And remember, the value of those assets doesn't change on the books with changing market conditions. You can't say that about the ubiquitous P/E ratio. That baby varies since earnings are strongly affected by different sets of accounting rules.

So a good way to use the price-to-book ratio is to compare your stock to the overall market. In December 2007, the S&P 500's price-to-book ratio was hovering around 2.5 to 3.0x. Where does your company fall? If its price-to-book ratio is lower, it might be a good value play. If it's higher, it could be more of a growth stock that the market is willing to put a premium on. Either way, use the ratio as a springboard for further investigation. Let a company's book value and corresponding price-to-book ratio help you test drive some stocks. Just don't let that one ratio make or break your decision.

The same goes for the Lamborghini. Just because the pedals are close together and your feet are too big doesn't mean you shouldn't buy the car.

It just means you should let me drive it, because my feet are smaller.

Growth Rate

A while ago my son and I were walking through town and saw a Porsche Cayman, which had just hit the streets. I got excited and said, "That car is hot!"

My super-bright kid, who was five at the time, responded, "But mommy, I just touched it and it's actually pretty cold."

I proceeded to explain that sometimes when things are really cool, we say they're hot. And he looked at me like I was the stupidest woman in the world. So I retracted my original statement and said, "That car is beautiful and I bet it goes really fast."

"Yeah, like 1,000 miles per hour!" he said.

The moral of this story is: There's clearly no place for slang when you're trying to teach someone the English language. Or any language, for that matter. So if you're going to invest in the stock world, you'd better understand its language as well. It's confusing enough sorting through the various abbreviations and acronyms thrown out daily by the pundits. And unfortunately, we've gotten very casual with language. Take *growth rate*. We hear it all the time. "The company's growth rate is 30 percent." "Its growth rate is expected to slow due to the weak dollar." What does it all mean?

What Are They Talking About?

The *growth rate* of a company generally refers to the rate of growth of its corporate earnings. When pundits mention a company's growth rate, they're generally referring to how a company's earnings have grown from one period to the next.

As a refresher, remember that earnings are basically revenues minus the cost of sales, operating expenses, taxes and deprecation, and the like, over a given period of time. They give investors an indication of the company's potential to expand.

Calculating an earnings growth rate is actually pretty simple: It's a basic percentage-change calculation, or what the accounting folks call an *analytical*. There are fabulous percent-change calculators all over the Internet. My personal choice is at www .percent-change.com. Or just go to your favorite stock site such as Yahoo! Finance or Google Finance and all the work is done for you.

Of course, you can always do it the old-fashioned way and pull out a calculator. Take the earnings-per-share number from the current period, subtract out the EPS number from the previous period, and then divide by the previous period's EPS. Multiply the final number by 100 to get a percentage.

So let's presume you're looking to crunch some numbers. Pull up Microsoft's (MSFT) quote. I like Google Finance for this stuff. It takes you to Reuters.com, but it has much clearer EPS and growth rate info. Enter your company's ticker symbol in Google Finance, and then scroll down to the Key Stats and Ratios section and click on "More Ratios from Reuters." If you scroll down the page, you'll actually find a growth rates section for both revenues and EPS. But to the left, you'll find an "Estimates" link in the list of options. Click on that to find all the EPS numbers you'll ever need. Look at the quarter-by-quarter numbers (make sure they're getting bigger) and check out the year-over-year (YOY) growth for the past 5 to 10 years. This will give you a feel for the path the company has been on.

You may also hear the talking heads on TV—yes, that would be me again—mention projected growth rates. Those include forecasted numbers, or future guesses, so you'll need to get out your crystal ball. But let's try to calculate a growth rate for June 30, 2009. That means we're looking for a "year-over-year projected earnings growth rate." According to Reuters.com, 2008's estimated EPS is 1.81. The 2009 estimate is 2.06. Since we're going forward to a future point in time, the 2008 number will be considered the previous period in our percentage calculation. So crunch (or drop the numbers into that cool percent-change calculator).

$$2.06 - 1.81/1.81 \times 100 = 13.8\%$$

That's easy enough. Now you know that the pros are expecting a 13.8 percent earnings growth from 2008 to 2009. That seems like good news. But remember, these numbers are useless unless you compare to the company's peers and get a perspective on what's normal.

Keep in mind that just like that "cool car," there are other interpretations of "growth rate." Some pros like to analyze revenue growth rate or sales growth rate—instead of the typical earnings growth rate, so they might mention a "growth rate" when talking about revenue or sales changes. That's fine—but they should be very clear about that in their discussion. A true pro is not going to use "growth" interchangeably between earnings and revenue. She'll make it clear to you that she's referring to a change in revenues *or* a change in earnings.

Knowing What's Important: A Case-by-Case Decision

While those are the most popular ratios used among analysts these days to dissect most stocks, there are certain numbers that are just more important to certain industries. For example, the inventory number is very important if you're looking at a home builder's stock because you can see whether the company is buying equipment, land to build on, and so on. The accounts receivable line is more important for a company that sells a product because you want to know that your company is getting paid.

Here are some more examples:

- For retail companies, look at their *same-store sales*. This statistic compares the sales of stores that have been open for a year or more. It helps you determine what portion of new sales came from sales growth and what portion are from the opening of new stores. Look also at the number of stores opening. Too many stores can mean the company has saturated the market and won't sell enough product to justify the stores, as was the case with as Starbucks (SBUX).
- In the technology world, profitability is key, so look at the *average selling price* of the products versus their costs. In addition, make sure the company is spending money on research and development because we all know how important it is to bring new products to the forefront.
- In the energy arena, while the fundamentals are important, the *geopolitical world* plays a large role here. The war in Iraq and hurricanes near oil pipelines all play a huge role in those companies' bottom lines, so stay abreast of the news.

Those are just three of many industry-specific metrics that analysts use to dissect companies. Get to know your company's industry by reading analysts' reports and news stories online from reputable sites such as the WSJ.com (i.e., the *Wall Street*

Journal), FOXBusiness.com, and Minyanville.com, to name a few. That extra reading will give you a feel for what the pros are looking at when they analyze your company.

Hard to Get Good Help

While I think everyone should crunch a few numbers now and then, there's really no need. Top-notch research firms have done it for you, and many of them now offer their reports on the Web for free. Read them and take comfort in the fact that you now know how that number was generated.

The proliferation of financial information on the Internet both helps and hurts. While it offers a bounty of information to the person trying to learn, that sometimes translates into overload and leads to frustration.

Be careful of what you read too. Not everything is policed, so make sure to pull up reliable sites and research reports. Shame on those business and financial news sites that don't explain their numbers. To just post a company's growth rate without proper explanation of how the number is calculated is irresponsible and almost sneaky. Stick to web sites you can trust because we need intelligent, well-informed investors for the market to behave properly.

Wrap-Up

This chapter discussed the price-to-earnings ratio, price-to-book ratio, and growth rate, three great metrics you can use to evaluate a stock:

- The *P/E ratio* basically tells you the price an investor is willing to pay for $1 of the company's earnings. If the P/E is $10, investors are willing to pay $10 for every $1 of earnings that the company generates.
- The *price-to-book ratio* measures what the market is willing to paying for your company's book value. A low price-to-book value could mean the stock is a bargain.

A higher price-to-book could mean the market is putting a premium on your stock.

- The *growth rate* of a company generally refers to the rate of growth of its corporate earnings. It tells you how a company's earnings have grown from one period to the next.

While this is by no means a complete list of metrics used to evaluate a stock, it's a great place to start. These ratios, coupled with your financial statement analysis, can help you make educated decisions.

Educated decisions will also prevent you from buying the Murciélago just because you look hot in it.

CHAPTER

11

The Ins and Outs of IPOs

Take it from a woman who has not gone to the bathroom alone in over six years: There is nothing more valuable than your privacy.

My children gather up their crayons and follow me just about every time I head to the bathroom. If by some chance the planets align properly, and I actually get in there alone and close the door, my three-year-old comes barreling in with some piece of groundbreaking news—"Mommy, Elmo's on TV!"

So I, for one, cherish my privacy, as fleeting as it may be.

Many entrepreneurs do, too. Not only do they get privacy in the bathroom, but they have the added luxury of being able to run their companies without the scrutiny of Wall Street or its discerning professionals. Privately held companies are owned by their founders or by a group of private investors. Your neighborhood pizza place is a privately held company, as is the local family-run funeral home business, and the nail salon down the street. Large companies can be private, too. Companies like IKEA, Domino's Pizza, and Hallmark Cards are all privately held.

While I don't expect you to take a company public anytime soon, I do think you should understand how—and why—some companies decide to relinquish their privacy for a ticker symbol on a major stock exchange, go through an *initial public offering*—an IPO—and become "publicly traded" instead.

In addition, when the market gets frenzied about upcoming IPOs, you'll hear the financial news talking about it. Take the recent IPO of VMware(VMW), a subsidiary of EMC, which provides virtualization solutions to aggregate multiple servers, storage infrastructure, and networks. The offer price was $29 when the stock went public on August 13, 2007. By December, the stock was trading in the mid-90s, making it one of the hot IPOs for that year.

Pop Goes the IPO

Let's assume that after much research, deliberation, and discussion, a privately held company decides to make the leap into the public arena. Now it must prepare for its initial public offering.

An IPO is basically the first day a company's stock trades in the marketplace. The company is now considered public, and its shares are available for investors to buy and sell, much like those of PepsiCo or Microsoft.

A company's IPO is much akin to its first birthday. Have you ever watched an IPO on one of the business channels? The CEO and management team stand at the podium—decked out in company swag—on the floor of the NYSE or the barely there podium at the Nasdaq, whichever exchange they opt to trade on. Everyone's jumping up and down like cheerleaders, and the CEO gets to slam the gavel on the podium like Judge Judy. Then it's off to the races. Employees plaster smiles on their faces, fingers crossed that stock goes up and stays up so they can send their kids to college *and* buy their dream house with the money they're going to make from this new issuance.

Going public does not always ensure a country club membership, but during the late 1990s tech bubble it did. Approximately 486 companies went public in 1999, according to IPOhome.com, compared to 234 in 2007, and many of those newly public company owners were barely old enough to buy the champagne they needed to toast the big day. That's because no one cared about whether the company had profits or potential; as long as it was technology-related, investors assumed the stock would soar. So investors dumped tons of money into these companies and helped young dot-com entrepreneurs take their tech dreams public.

It was nutty. Trust me. I was a financial journalist at TheStreet.com during that frenetic era, watching stocks like VA Linux Systems (LNUX). It jumped 700 percent points on its first day of trading in December 1999, hitting almost $250 a share.

VA Linux was hardly an anomaly. I can tell you tons of similar stories. Take Priceline.com (PCLN), the online airline ticket retailer that uses William Shatner as its spokesperson. The company went public in March 1999. The stock *priced* at $16, marketspeak for where it started trading on its first day. I guess a lot of traders are *Star Trek* fans because it soared to $69 on its first day. That's a 331 percent pop, one of the best first-day IPO performers ever. At the end of its first year of trading, Priceline was still up 407 percent from its offering price.

It's no surprise that the 1990s turned the average buy-and-hold investors into avid IPO watchers, seduced by the triple-digit gains many new issues posted on their first day of trading.

As the cliché goes, what goes up must come down. The tech bubble burst by the end of 2000; high fliers such as Priceline tanked to under $10. Same with VA Linux, which wasn't financially strong enough to justify its $250 stock price anyway. By April 2000, it was down to $30. These days, the company, which recently changed its name to SourceForge, trades under $2. I'm not kidding.

Not only did I report on these wild rides, I had a seat on the rollercoaster. TheStreet.com (TSCM) decided to follow its tech-brethren and go public on May 21, 1999. The stock started trading at $17 and shot to more than $70 on the first day. Those of us that had been long-time employees were given a small financial stake in the IPO, and man, did we think we were going to hit it *big!* I got the Lamborghini dealer on the phone that day and was already contemplating colors, but, of course, that kind of overnight wealth happened only to the people we wrote about. TheStreet's stock swallowed its first-day pop and fell to

$26 a month later. By August 1999 it was around $18 and by the by the end of 2000, it was hovering around $3. These days it trades around $10.

Clearly, the Lamborghini was not an option.

Interview with Dave Kansas

I met Dave Kansas back in 1998, when he was editor-in-chief of a little start-up financial web site called TheStreet.com. He hired me as a reporter and basically gave me a front-row seat to the tech bubble.

Dave, in addition to being a great editor, helped take TheStreet.com public in 1999. He went on to run the Money and Business section of the *Wall Street Journal* and has most recently left to start up another web site called FiLife.com, a personal finance site aimed at people 18–40. Backed by IAC and Barry Diller, Dave will make that successful, too.

Dave has become a dear friend and mentor, and I wanted to pick his brain on the IPO process. Read on for some of his thoughts.

Tracy: How did you get involved with an IPO and what did you love about the process?

Dave: As a director at TheStreet.com, I was involved in the process from the very beginning. There's a lot of stuff I didn't do, namely, legal legwork and the road show where the IPO is marketed to potential investors. One fun thing was ringing "the bell" at the Nasdaq when we started trading. Then we watched our stock moon-shot from its opening price of $17 to more than $70 on the first day. That was crazy. Eventually, of course, the price settled at much lower levels.

T: What's the single most important thing investors don't know about investing in IPOs?

D: The "price" of the IPO, especially hot IPOs, isn't often available to regular investors. The IPO is often sold to institutions, like mutual funds, and these buyers will start trading the IPO. Not every IPO is hot, so this isn't always a problem for the regular investor. But in the case of hot IPOs, if you can't access the initial offered price, then it's often wiser to wait and let the animal spirits settle before making an investment.

T: What's the most dangerous thing an investor can fail to realize about IPOs?

D: A lot of IPOs, especially in the biotech and technology space, can represent untested companies. Read the prospectus and understand the financial health of a company before putting your cash on the line. A lot of people don't do this homework, and that can lead to dangerous mistakes.

T: What's the single most important method for getting rich?

D: Hard work is important. Having a game plan is important. But it's very difficult to get rich without taking risks. You can diminish the downside of risks by doing homework—studying the financials of an investment before buying, for instance. The reality is that if getting rich were a risk-free exercise, everyone would be rich. Many rich people lose their fortunes because they become addicted to risk and can't settle for what they've achieved.

T: Name the three investing information sources you use the most.

D: The Wall Street Journal Online, Yahoo! Finance, and *The Economist.*

A Beneficial Blow

TheStreet.com was not alone on its IPO slalom. One-fifth of the shares that began public trading in the 1990s have declined more than 90 percent from their offering price. That's mostly because so many of those companies should never have been sold to public investors to begin with. Many of those companies had no money, no product, and no future. But Wall Street was too busy checking its bank account and didn't even notice. Investors were reminded of a valuable lesson—the IPO can be risky business.

As a result, the IPO market went underground for a bit. As a matter of fact, only 83 companies went public in 2001 (see Table 11.1). But as the market turned itself around, so did the IPO world. In 2004, 216 companies went public. The trend has held steady over the years, and 2007 kept pace, finishing off the year with 234 IPOs. This time, however, investors were more discriminating. We rarely saw stocks popping over 300 percent on the first day of trading anymore (see Table 11.2).

You can still find some quick moneymakers. Take Baidu .com, the Chinese version of Google. Its stock ran up 239 percent on the first day it went public back in early August 2005. But that's not the norm. These days, the average IPO only jumps up around 11 percent on the first day, according to IPOhome .com, although more recently VMware ratcheted up 76 percent to $124, thanks to Wall Street's excitement for the software maker and for an IPO in general. The stock has come down and was hovering around $77 in January 2008.

Despite the occasional anomaly, the IPO world is still a much more rational place to be these days, mainly because we're not seeing dot-coms going public. More stable sectors such as health care and energy are doing more of the offerings and doing quite well. Of the 46 health care IPOs in 2007, the average return has been around 8 percent, with some, such as WuXi PharmaTech (WX), the leading China-based contract research organization for U.S. pharmas and biotechs, returning around 98 percent since its August 8, 2007, IPO date.

For the most part, the pace of the IPO market is not nearly as frenetic as it was in the late 1990s and most of the companies participating in IPOs actually have earnings even before they hit the exchanges. Does this mean you should you be investigating IPOs for you portfolio?

Hardly. These things are very risky. But if you can get your hands on the right information, there could actually be a place for them. Either way, it's important you understand the process of how a company goes from small neighborhood storefront to global conglomerate. Remember, Steve Jobs started

Table 11.1 2007 IPO Review: Tech Bubble to the Present

	1999	2000	2001	2002	2003	2004	2005	2006	2007
Number of deals	486	406	83	70	68	216	194	198	234
Total proceeds (billions)	$93	$97	$41	$24	$15	$43	$34	$43	$54
Average deal size (millions)	$191	$240	$491	$338	$224	$198	$175	$217	$229

Source: Renaissance Capital LLC (www.IPOhome.com).

Table 11.2 Average IPO Returns

	1999	2000	2001	2002	2003	2004	2005	2006	2007
Total return	276%	−18%	16%	3%	28%	34%	18%	26%	13%

Source: Renaissance Capital LLC (www.IPOhome.com).

his computer business in his garage. Bill Gates started his phenomenon in his college dorm room. These guys went from small-time to worldwide, all with an IPO.

So let's walk through the mechanics. Once you're comfortable with the concepts, we'll decide if these are the right stocks for your portfolio.

Knowing When to Make the Move from Public to Private

As a private company, owners can make their decisions without having to answer to public oversight boards or shareholders. They are free to do what they want, when they want, and have very few guidelines to follow.

Publicly traded companies, on the other hand, have to present their financial statements to their shareholders every quarter and then have to create a big yearly wrap-up of all their financial information in their annual report. These days, preparing those reports is not easy. You remember the Enron explosion back in 2001? The company's big shots were playing around with the numbers, pocketing profits for themselves and misleading shareholders. As a result of that horrific finagling, Congress passed the Sarbanes-Oxley Act of 2002 to protect investors from that ever happening again. Well, those rules are pretty stringent and many public companies spend millions of dollars just to stay in compliance.

Among the many new rules outlined by Sarbanes-Oxley are stricter disclosures within company financial statements and ethical guidelines to which senior financial officers must adhere, as well as some serious consequences of activities that are deemed criminal by the act. Sounds like a lot, but I have to tell you, as cumbersome as they may be, we have not had another Enron scandal since, so you have to give them some props.

On the flip side, private companies do not have to follow these rules and have more freedom in their reporting standards. But with that freedom comes personal funding. Privately held companies have to come up with the money they need to keep the business going on their own (or they beg and borrow from family members). That's because a private company does not get money from shareholders like public companies do. Remember, when you buy a share of stock in a public company, you invest your money in its business in exchange for a piece of its future profits. By making that trade, the company gets to use your money to grow the business.

Privately held companies have to dip into their own pockets or bring in partners or banks for funding. When that money runs out, many private companies are often willing to give up the perks of freedom in exchange for more funding. So whether they need the money to cover the day-to-day bills, to pursue some acquisitions, or to pay down debt, getting more financing is generally the driving factor behind an initial public offering. Plus, trading on a major stock exchange carries a ton of cachet. Having a publicly trading stock is basically like saying "Happy birthday! You've arrived!"

Take That IPO on the Road

As the tech bubble proved, not every company is fit to go public. A qualified company must have high-growth prospects, offer an innovative product or service, and meet some rigorous financial requirements. Remember, the company is going public because it wants people like you and me to buy its stock. So if it doesn't have solid credentials, we'll just take our money elsewhere.

If a company believes it's got what it takes, the first thing it needs to do is hire an *underwriter.* Bankers such as Goldman Sachs, Morgan Stanley, or Lehman Brothers work with the company to make sure it has the necessary legal documentation and the proper financial support to go public. These requirements are steep. Most underwriters are looking for annual revenues of around $10 to $20 million with profits around $1 million. In addition, they want to know that the company will continue to grow at around 25 percent a year over the next five to seven years. That's why you don't see too many nail salons trading on the NYSE these days.

One of the underwriters' biggest jobs is to help the company determine its initial stock price, or *offering price*. It's important that they get it right because they have to help sell the stock once it's public. If they price the stock too high and no one buys it, the underwriters will be forced to lower the price. The difference between the original price and the new lower one will come out of their pockets and they certainly don't want that to happen.

Once the underwriters are chosen, attorneys are hired. Together, they help the company create its *registration statement*. That document discloses all the pertinent information relating to a company's operations, securities, management, and the purpose of the offering. Before the company can go public, that document must be approved by the Securities and Exchange Commission(SEC), the agency responsible for administering federal securities laws in the United States.

The SEC will read the registration statement—we dissect this statement in a moment—and may request additional information if necessary. The company must supply all that extra information before the document can be finalized.

Once all the paperwork is complete, the bankers hit the streets—literally—and try to promote the stock to potential investors.

This traveling PR party has been dubbed the *road show*. It's a grueling whirlwind multicity world tour that usually lasts a week or two. The company's management team goes to a new city just about every day to meet with prospective investors and explain its business plan. Typical U.S. stops on the road show include New York, San Francisco, Boston, Chicago, and Los Angeles. If appropriate, international destinations like London or Hong Kong may also be included.

A management's road show performance plays a huge role in determining the success of its IPO. To start, the road show's guest list is solely comprised of institutional (read: high-roller) investors who have the money to buy *really* big chunks of stock. If the company can convince the institutional investors that it has a strong, solid future, the investors will want to buy a significant amount of stock, which is the ultimate goal.

People like you and me who are looking for a place to invest some money for retirement are *not* invited to this private party. We don't have nearly enough cash to invest.

These road show meetings are only face-to-face at this point, and any information discussed generally stays among the invitees. The SEC has proposed new rules that will make it easier for companies to broadcast these road shows via the Web. Until then, we're in the dark until the company comes public. That's part of the reason why playing the IPO market is unfair to the average investor.

Once the road show is over, the official *prospectus* is printed. We'll cover this in more detail in the next section.

Sorting through the S-1

Before we get into *how* to invest in an IPO, you need to decide if you even *want* the company in your portfolio.

Do you understand the company's business? Do you know if it makes any money? You should, and reading the prospectus is the best way to gather that information.

The SEC requires companies that want to go public to file a registration statement (called Form S-1). This is supposed to give potential investors full disclosure of all the "material facts" you would need to make an important investment decision. I say "supposed to" because the lawyers write this thing. That means its chock-full of jargon and those bunched-up words like *heretofore* and *therewithal.* Leo Tolstoy's *War and Peace* might actually be an easier read, but if you're thinking about investing in an IPO, you have to tackle it.

Finding Prospects in the Prospectus

The prospectus is found in the Form S-1: Registration Statement. It's where the company describes the important facts about its business operations, financial condition, and management.

We talked about reading a prospectus back in Chapter 4, "Mutual Funds and ETFs," where I highlighted the important parts you needed to read to make a good mutual fund decision and then told you not to bother reading the rest (unless you had nothing better to do). In that instance, it was more efficient to scour the Web for the gory details because journalists most likely ripped the mutual fund prospectus to shreds and wrote about it. Remember, I'm about efficiency.

In this case, however, you have to read a bit more of an IPO's prospectus mainly because it's so new that reporters haven't had a chance to tear it apart yet. But by no means do you have to read the whole thing because these documents can be well over 100 pages.

Still, the Web can help. There is a plethora of dirt out there on most IPOs. Start with a site such as IPOhome.com and click the IPO Research link. That page lists all upcoming IPOs and links directly to available S-1 forms. A ton of free information is available on the site, and for a mere $30 you can purchase IPOhome.com's own report that dissects the prospectus for you.

Next, check out the IPO blogs to get a feel for what the traders are buzzing about. You should take any information you read on a blog with the proverbial grain of salt; but there are some smart people out there, so be a voyeur. Aside from the blog at IPOhome.com, I like 247wallst.com and the IPO/Offerings page at dealbook.blogs.nytimes.com. Otherwise, just enter "IPO" at Google Blog Search (blogsearch.google.com). You'll get some good grist from investors. Just remember that blogs are not policed, so fact-check your information.

Even with the Internet, you still need to read parts of the prospectus. I know you don't have time to read the whole thing, so just flip to the important parts.

On the front page you'll find the company's name, anticipated ticker symbol, number of shares offered, price range, and insider buying and selling. At the bottom of the page are the managing underwriters, arrayed from left to right in order of importance. Do you recognize the names? Are they respected national or regional firms? You're hoping for big names, like Goldman Sachs, Morgan Stanley, and Thomas Weisel, that will bring credibility to the deal.

Next, concentrate on the following four main sections:

- Prospectus Summary
- Risk Factors
- Use of Proceeds
- Management's Discussion and Analysis.

In the Prospectus Summary, you'll find a basic description of the company, the hopes and dreams of its founders, how the company fits into the industry, its achievements, and its strategy for growth. This can include some serious hyperbole, so be skeptical, but at least you'll get a description of what the company does and how it makes its money.

The Prospectus Summary also includes a rundown of how many shares are being offered. Be wary of the number of "option shares" being offered. We'll dive into options in the next chapter, but basically an option gives a person the right to purchase a share of stock at a set price that is generally below the offering price. Options are issued to company executives as part of their compensation as an incentive to perform well. Look at the price and number of options. Very low priced options are just free money to insiders, hardly incentives. You don't want to see too much of that.

The Risk Factors section is very important because it basically tells you what could go wrong. It presents the company in the worst light possible. If the company is a young start up, a ton of stuff could blow up. In all likelihood, the company probably hasn't made any money yet and may even have losses. Can it achieve or maintain profitability? Use your gut here because the company may be so new that it has little sales history and/or very few clients, so it's sometimes difficult to predict how well its product will sell.

Then there's the competition. If the company is a latecomer in an area already populated with large, established companies, that's clearly a big risk. Same goes for being reliant on a few customers, a geographic location, or a particular time of year for sales. If you see the word *litigation* in the Risk Factors section of a prospectus, panic. The last thing you want to see is a company coming public with pending lawsuits.

The Use of Proceeds section explains how the company will spend the money it raises through the public offering. Is it simply going public to pay off some debt, or is it using the money to reinvest in the company and help it grow? Clearly, you want to see that the company plans to use the proceeds to expand the business or for R&D. Be very wary if the company actually has the nerve to say it has no specific plans for using the proceeds at this time. It begs the question: Why is it going public in the first place? To offer management IPO shares and make them rich? No thanks.

Next, read Management's Discussion and Analysis. We tackled this in Chapter 5, so by now you know it's a great summary of what the company does, where its revenue comes from, how it recognizes revenue, what its expenses are, and what its significant accounting policies are.

From there, continue to dissect the financials using the techniques you learned in Chapters 6 and 7. Apply them to your company's prospectus and you'll have a real good idea of the company's financial meat—or lack thereof.

Getting a Ticket to the Hottest Party in Town

On July 7, 2007, actress Eva Longoria and basketball player Tony Parker got married in Paris, France. They said their "I do's" at the Saint Germain L'Auxerrois cathedral, where the guest list included the rest of the *Desperate Housewives* cast, Sheryl Crow, Michael Douglas, Catherine Zeta-Jones, and Jamie Foxx. It was arguably one of the most coveted tickets in Hollywood.

And it was probably easier to get an invitation to that party than to get pre-IPO shares for your portfolio.

Pre-IPO shares are reserved for the people on the inside. While the main goal is to sell shares to the big institutional buyers, the company's management and its bankers want in on those cheap shares, too. So the bankers purposely set aside some pre-IPO shares for themselves, the company's management, and their "closest friends and family members."

Now remember, these pre-IPO shares are actually cheaper than what the stock will start trading at on its first day. So let's say the stock is set to price at $19 on opening day. If would not be unreasonable for the bankers to offer those exact shares for, say, $5 to the big fat institutions. So even if the stock doesn't move on its first day of trading, the institutional investors have already made loads of money. Imagine if it pops. Let's say the stock jumps to $60 a share. That's an instant $55 profit, albeit on paper. That's exactly why the bankers and management— and everyone else in the world—want those pre-IPO shares.

Many companies going public also have these so-called "friends and family" programs. In addition to holding shares aside for themselves and management, the bankers also give the company a certain number of shares that it can distribute to its friends and family. The CEO, for example, can buy shares for his mom at those ridiculously cheap prices. The idea is that the stock will go up and his mom will make even more money than the rest of the world.

No surprise, that doesn't always happen. I got my mom those insider shares back when TheStreet.com went public. While she paid next to nothing for the shares, she still would've been better off dropping the money in the collection basket at church. At least she would've gotten a tax deduction for it.

I'm Not a Friend or a Family Member!

If you're not employed by a company going public or don't happen to be the banker's favorite aunt, can you still get yourself some IPO shares?

In most instances, the answer is no. But here are some options.

The most straightforward way to get shares is to have an account with the bankers working on the deal. If you have a brokerage account with, say, Morgan Stanley, and they're doing the work for an IPO you like, your Morgan Stanley broker may be able to get you some shares. And the bigger your account, the more eager they will be to get you some shares.

Check out your broker's web site to see the deals they're working on. If that doesn't work, you have no choice but to buy the stock on the open market like everyone else. Just not immediately.

40 Days and 40 Nights

No one wants to wait for anything these days, but remember that the second a stock starts trading on its preferred exchange, it officially becomes a publicly traded company and, in theory, should be around for a while.

So sit back and watch the stock for a bit. Use the time to confirm that the company has substance. If the stock is a loser, it will quickly hit the skids and you'll be glad you heeded my warning. Then follow the bouncing ball for a few months. There are two monumental moments in a young stock's life that cause the stock price to artificially jump around for a bit. The first starts about 40 days after its IPO. That's because there is a period of "silence" right after an IPO is priced. Yep, silence. That means the bankers have to keep their mouths shut about the stock for about 40 days. That means no talking to the press, potential investors, or the guys at the gym.

This is totally contrary to what the bankers *want* to do, of course. Remember, these guys got those cheapo pre-IPO shares, so they have a vested interest in getting people to invest in the company so the stock price goes up. That's exactly why the SEC insists on a "quiet period" after every IPO. The sole purpose of the quiet period is to send the cheerleaders to the sidelines for a bit and allow the stock time to actually trade on its own merit. That means the bankers who took the company public can't talk about the stock to anybody for at least 40 days and sometimes more, depending on the deal.

But the minute the 40-day period ends, prepare for the blitz of positive news ratings and glowing research reports, which will most likely send the stock price up. There will be enough people out there who are gullible enough to believe all this good news and buy the stock—but not you! You're smart enough to know now that you need to wait until that media frenzy settles down.

So check the prospectus and know the date of your IPO's quiet period expiration. Or what's simpler, go to IPOhome.com, which lists all upcoming quiet period expirations in the Marketwatch page of its site under Calendars (www.ipohome.com/market watch/quiet.asp).

Happy Half-Year Birthday

I love this half-year birthday concept. My birthday is in August. (Hello, fellow Leos!) So I never had a birthday party in school when I was a kid. Even worse, when the summer hit and it actually came time for my big day, all my friends were usually on vacation with their families. I could barely drum up enough kids to have a party.

Thankfully, the party industry got industrious and realized they were losing money on people like me. So this whole concept of half-year birthdays began. My daughters are also summer babies, so they get to have in-school birthday parties at their half-year mark. That's genius. Lazy mothers like me just go along with it and make a full-blown half-year fiesta out of it. If my kid is celebrating her birthday in school, why not keep the festivities going and take 25 little girls to the nearest play gym so they can run around, have pizza and cake, and get ridiculously expensive goody bags?

A newly IPO-ed stock gets to celebrate its half-year birthday, too, only it's not nearly as fun. As a matter of fact, the stock generally tanks at that point. That's because this six-month milestone marks the end of the *lockup period*. The lockup period is imposed by the investment bankers, forcing the folks who got those ridiculously cheap shares to hold them for a requisite amount of time.

Here's how that works: Remember how all those lucky friends and family members got ridiculously cheap shares before the IPO? And in our example at the beginning of this section, we presumed that the pre-IPO shares priced at $19 and then assumed the stock ran up to $60. If you were one of the chosen few who got those shares at that friends and family discount of, say, $5, wouldn't you just love to sell those shares at $60, take your money and head off to Tahiti?

Definitely!

Which is exactly why you can't.

If you did, everyone would and the market would be flooded with shares that no one wanted. That would increase the supply of available shares, and when the supply of anything goes up, the price comes down.

The *last* thing the investment bankers want is for the share price to drop. That's why they typically require the insiders who got those super-cheap shares to hold them for a minimum 180 days after the IPO.

The second that 180-day lockup period is over, investors are free to sell those shares. As long as the stock is up, you will most certainly see massive selling. Clearly, that hurts the stock price because the supply will be increasing without a corresponding increase in demand.

The last thing you want to do is buy the stock near its lockup period expiration day. Be sure you know your stock's half-birthday—and you should look it up, as bankers have full discretion to make it another day. The actual lockup expiration day can be found in the prospectus, but I think that's a big pain so I use IPOhome.com. They have a listing of the upcoming lockup expirations in that same Calendar section (www.ipohome.com/marketwatch/lockup.asp).

Leave the Stock, Take the Fund

Another way to dabble in the IPO world is to consider buying a mutual fund that specializes in them. There are a bunch of funds out there that invest directly in the IPO world. For straight-up exposure, try Renaissance Capital's IPO Plus Fund (IPOSX), which focuses solely on IPOs and was up about 5 percent in 2007, in line with the S&P 500.

Other funds focus more on the small-cap world, which is where many of the IPOs germinate. So check out Morningstar .com for updates on mutual funds that focus on IPOs.

Wrap-Up

Playing the IPO game is very exclusive and very risky. While IPO gains can be huge, especially if you get those pre-IPO shares, it's important to remember that's its easier to get invited to a Hollywood wedding than to play in this arena. That's because you're playing against the big boys, who have the money, the information, and the connections they need to get in the game. So you should either wait until the stock's early gyrations are over before you buy it, or just skip the party altogether. The last thing you want to do is to fall for those novice mistakes of buying high and then watching the stock fall because the big guys have hit an expiration day that allows them to dump their shares.

Whether you decide to invest or not, it's still really important to understand the so-called "birth" of a stock. Because once you know how a stock comes to life, it's much easier to understand how to rip it to shreds.

CHAPTER 12

Options and Futures

Moving beyond trading stocks, bonds, mutual funds, and exchange-traded funds for a moment, there is an entire universe of professionals who trade options and futures. These products allow traders to place bets on what's going to happen in the future. It can be a risky game. Novices need not apply. But the beauty is that we can be voyeurs in this high-paced world and learn a ton about the sentiment of the market.

An Introduction to Options

Options traders have their own vernacular. Just the other day, I had a trader mention the GS 260 and 260 calls to me.

What?

Then he mentioned how the traders watch the option activity to judge the price movements of a stock. Are the puts more active than the calls?

Is that a good thing?

Understanding what the options traders are doing can really help you get a sense of how the market feels about your stock. We're going to dive into the options world now. We'll walk through how to use options on your stock holdings and what you can learn from their trades. We'll then touch on the so-called "futures market." That's basically where traders place bets on what the price of commodities such as corn and oil will be a few months out. Now, by no means do I want you to start trading futures. If you do, all power to you. I do want you to be able to watch these markets from the sidelines and understand what they're telling you.

Let's figure out your options. (Sorry, I couldn't resist the pun.)

Talking the Options Talk

Options are similar to insurance. They are contracts that give you the right, but not the obligation, to buy or sell an underlying asset at a specific price on or before a certain date. Here's how they work.

Let's say you're in the market for an old-school 1980 Corvette—white with red leather interior and T-tops, for argument's sake. You find one that you love and the price is right; but you really need to have it checked out by a pro. So you give the owner a nonrefundable $500 to secure your right to buy the car at his current asking price for the next two weeks. That gives you enough time to get a good mechanic to check it out without having to worry that the owner is going to jack up his price.

If the car turns out to be a lemon, you lose $500—but at least you didn't buy a hunk of junk.

But let's say the car's immaculate. The owner realizes this and raises the price to other prospective buyers. Since you have an insurance contract with him, you're still locked in at the original price. In fact, you're so excited that you buy it before your two weeks is up. In essence, that insurance policy bought you some time to make a sound decision and protected you from any downside.

That's pretty much how equity options work. In our example, the "option" was the money used to hold the price ($500). The underlying asset was the fabulous Corvette that's now in your garage.

In the equity option world, the underlying asset is usually a stock or an index. And options are used as a way to hedge or insure a stock from a decline. (Some people use options to speculate market moves, but that's fodder for another day.)

Here's the technical definition: *An option is a contract that gives the buyer the right, but not the obligation, to buy or sell a stock at a specific price on or before a certain date.* Since you're not obligated to *do* anything, you can always let the option expire. It then becomes worthless and you lost the money you used to buy the option. People who buy options are called *holders,* and people who sell options are called *writers.*

There are two types of options: calls and puts.

A *call* gives the holder the right to buy an asset at a certain price within a specific period of time. Calls are similar to having a "long" position on a stock. Whether you hold the call or just hold the stock, you want the stock price to go up.

Call buyers hope the stock's price is going to increase before the option expires, though. So, as a simple example, if Microsoft (MSFT) is trading at $35 today and you think it's going to hit $45, you could buy an option on the stock to buy the shares at $40. When the stock hits $42, you'd exercise your option to buy at $40 and save yourself $2. If Microsoft falls, you'd let your option expire worthless and all you lost is the measly price of the option.

A *put* gives the holder the right to sell an asset at a certain price within a specific period of time. Puts are very similar to having a "short" position on a stock because both trades are betting the stock will fall. But again, put buyers hope the stock price falls before the option expires. If Microsoft falls to $32, but you have an option that says you can sell your shares at $34, you just saved yourself $2.

Now let's dissect an option quote. Take the MSFT Oct 40 calls. That ticker is quoting a call option on Microsoft. "Oct" is short for October, the month the option expires. Options expire on the third Friday of the month, so this particular option expires on the third Friday of October. If it were an MSFT Nov 40 call, it would expire on the third Friday of November.

In this example, "40" is the *strike* or *exercise* price. That's the price you're able to buy the underlying shares for. So if you buy an MSFT Oct 40 call, you're buying the right to buy Microsoft shares at $40. If Microsoft hits $42 in early October before your option expires, you're psyched because you have an option that lets you buy those exact shares for only $40. If Microsoft doesn't hit $40 before expiration day, you'll just let the option expire worthless and walk away. On the other hand, if you're a put holder, you would have the right to sell Microsoft at $40. If Microsoft slipped to $34, you could exercise your option and sell your shares at $40. Yippee!

Each listed option is known as a *contract* and represents 100 shares of a company's stock. To figure out your option's actual cost, or *premium,* you must multiply the option price by 100. If our MSFT Oct 40 call had a hypothetical price of $2, the actual cost of that option would be $200 since all listed options represent 100 shares of stock.

How are you doing? I know this is heady stuff, but just a few more definitions to get you in the know.

An option is *in-the-money* when its strike price is less than the stock's actual price. So if Microsoft is trading at $42, and you have a call option that says you can buy shares at $40, you're psyched. You can "exercise" your option and buy the shares at $40. You now have a $2 gain on your books. So "in-the-money" means you're sitting in money!

If a put option is in-the-money, its strike price is greater than the stock's actual price. So let's say Microsoft is trading at $36 and you buy a put option with a $34 strike price. If Microsoft falls to $32, you can exercise your option and sell your shares at $34. So you only lost a $2, as opposed to $4 if you didn't have the option. You're "in more money" than the rest of us who sold at $32.

When an option is *at-the-money,* its strike equals the share's market price, so it's a wash.

An *out-of-the-money* option means your hedge didn't work. In this instance, the strike price on your call is greater than the actual share price. So if the strike on your call is $42 and Microsoft is at $39, you wouldn't exercise. Your put is out-of-the-money if its strike is below the market price. Let's say the strike price on your put is at $37. With Microsoft at $39, you wouldn't want to sell your shares for $37. So you just let it expire and move on. Thankfully, all you lost was the option price.

For more information on any of these terms, check out the education sections of the Chicago Board Options Exchange (CBOE) at www.cboe.com/LearnCenter/OptionsInstitute1 .aspx and the Chicago Mercantile Exchange (CME) at www .cme.com/edu.

Walking the Options Walk

Now that you know the lingo, it's time to figure out how to use these things. Remember, options are like insurance—insurance that can make you some serious money. In this section, we discuss using options to protect your underlying stock holdings. There are two main strategies that a stockholder can use: protective puts and covered calls.

Protective Puts If you're afraid your company is about to announce some bad news and the stock will take a hit, or you think maybe an upcoming presidential election is going to hurt it a bit but still believe in its long-term potential, consider buying a put to protect your existing gains. This is known as a *protective put*. If you own the asset and want to keep it, but you're nervous that something might happen in the future, consider a protective put.

Another reason to buy a put on stock that you already own is to extend your holding period for tax purposes. We'll get into the tax implications of trading more in Chapter 13. For now, know that if you own the stock for less than a year and sell it at a gain, you will owe tax at your regular ordinary income tax rate, which could be as high as 35 percent. But if you hold the stock for at least a year, then sell it, that gain will be taxed at the preferential 15 percent capital gains rate. A put option could again help you secure your profits until that time is up. That way, you're still bullish on the underlying stock.

In either case, the options folks say you're buying a protective put because you're limiting your losses but still allowing for maximum upside. Remember, a put gives the holder the right to *sell* an asset at a certain price within a specific period of time. If the stock price falls below the strike price before expiration of the option, you could exercise your put option and sell your shares at the strike price. If the stock price jumps up above the strike price, you would just let the option expire worthless and the only money you lost was the option price—or your insurance premium.

Here's an example. Let's say you own Procter & Gamble (PG), which has been hovering around $63, and you believe the market is shifting into a bearish phase. However, since you bought the stock at $53 back in April, you'd like to protect your profits and try to hold the issue for at least a year before you sell.

So consider buying the PG Apr $60 put, which costs around $1.90. This, in essence, ensures you a sale price of $58.10, which is the strike price—$60—minus the premium paid—$1.90. Remember, each option covers 100 shares, so you'll need to cough up $190 to protect 100 shares of Procter & Gamble. But that put would have enabled you to sell your shares at a strike price of $60 if the stock falls.

Let's imagine the stock does tank and is down to $58 by next April. You decide to exercise your put before expiration day, the third Friday of the month. So instead of selling each share for $58, which is what it's trading for in the marketplace, and realizing a $5 gain on each share ($58 − $53), your put allows you to sell for $60 and bump your gain to $5.10 per share. That's because your profit is equal to the strike price less the stock purchase price, less the premium paid. In our example, that's $60 − $53 − $1.90 = $5.10. So you are securing a $5.10 profit per share.

Bravo! Your insurance worked.

If, however, the stock kept going up in price, you'd just let the option expire and be out $190. But at least you would be able to sleep at night.

Covered Calls   What if you think the stock is going to be flat for a bit, even though you see big upside potential in the long term? Maybe you think the market will be at a standstill because of current market conditions. Consider selling a call and getting paid while you wait for the stock to hit its price.

Remember, a call gives the holder the right to buy an asset at a certain price within a specific period of time. In this instance, you could write (sell) a call option on your existing shares. Options guys call this a *covered call* because you already own the shares to "cover" your obligation if the option gets exercised. If you buy the stock at the same time you write the call contract, folks in the know call that a "buy-write."

Let's say you bought Procter & Gamble and believe the stock will trade relatively flat in the short term. You decide to sell a call option on Procter & Gamble for $65 at, say, $2. You immediately get the premium—the $2—from the option sale. If Procter & Gamble doesn't move before expiration day, the option expires worthless, but you have two extra dollars in your pocket, thanks to the option you sold.

But what if Procter & Gamble rises to $68? The option you sold would most likely be exercised, and you'd have to give up your shares. You'll have to sell them to the option holder for $65 (the strike price of the option), even though they're trading on the open market for $68. But all is not lost—you still have the $2 premium from the sale of the option. This caps your effective sell price at $67, which is the strike plus the premium collected from the sale of the call option.

Your overall profit, therefore, is the difference between the strike price and your original purchase price, plus the premium from the option:

$$\$65 - \$53 + \$2 = \$14$$

You preserved most of that gain with your option.

Check the Expiration Date: Options Expiration Week

Now let's focus on what you can learn just by watching the options market and its monthly revelry, also known as *options expiration week*. Believe it or not, that can help you better understand the overall market.

Remember, there are two basic equity types of options—calls and puts. A call gives you the right to buy an asset at a certain price within a specific period of time. Buyers of calls hope that the stock will increase substantially before the option expires because their option gives them the right to buy those same shares at a lower price. Buying a put option gives you the right to sell a stock at a certain price within a specific period of time. It's a lot like taking a short position. When you buy a put, you're betting the price of the stock will fall before the option expires so that you can sell it at your locked-in higher price.

You can't hold an option forever like you can a stock. As a matter of fact, on the third Friday of every month, options actually expire and become worthless. In the days leading up to that Friday of expiration week, options traders need to decide whether to exercise that put or call or just let it expire worthless and walk away from the deal.

Pump Up the Volume

All this decision making can translate into increased volume in both the options and equity markets. That's because there's extra buying and selling, thanks to the deadline. For proof of this increased volume, check out the Options Clearing Corp. web site at www.theocc.com during week expiration week. You can watch the option volume increase each day until it peaks on Friday.

The lesson here is to be aware that there's activity going on and try to understand what it is, especially if there are options being traded on a stock you hold. The Chicago Board Options Exchange (CBOE) web site (cboe.com/default.aspx) will tell you that detail. Figure out what people are buying. If you see an increase in calls on your stock, it may be a sign that people are expecting the stock price to rise. If there's an exceptional amount of puts out there, be concerned that traders are essentially shorting your stock because they're expecting the price to go lower. Granted, options traders buy options for many different reasons, and tons of them trade options without ever owning the underlying stock. A trader could buy a put (a bet that the price is going to fall) on a high-flying stock to hedge against a totally different position. So just use these metrics as a gauge.

With the increase in options volume comes a similar increase in volume in the equity market. Don't forget, options are a contract to buy or sell a stock at a specific price. If traders decide to exercise those options, they may buy or sell the underlying stock at the same time. That creates an increase in volume in the equities market, and many of the TV talking heads, yours truly included, often refer to that during options expiration week. This extra volume brings out the buyers and sellers. So you may see an increase in trading from large position holders such as the institutions and mutual funds. If they want to buy or sell a large chunk of stock, they'll get a better price when the volume is high because that means there are more buyers or sellers in the marketplace.

Check the volume on your stock during expiration week as well. In addition, be on the lookout for *triple witching,* an industry term that refers to the four times a year that futures options expire on the same day as equity options.

Futures options, which we'll cover next, expire once every quarter. On the third Friday of March, June, September, and December, not only are regular options expiring, but some outstanding futures contracts will be expiring as well. So expect the volume of everything to be even higher that week.

Use the Futures Market to Foresee Market

You wake up, turn on one of the financial networks, and the first thing you hear is a pundit reporting on the futures market, saying things like:

> Nothing can withstand this futures onslaught, so you should keep your eyes out for individual stocks that could still do well in this environment.

> It won't matter until the company is acquired because no one wants a company that has natural gas as a business when the natural-gas futures are trending down.

It's early and you're still trying to get yourself into the present, never mind the future. You're not really sure if they're talking about stocks or space travel. After you blink your eyes a few times and have a cup of coffee, you realize they're talking about the overnight *stock* futures market.

Morning television and boardwalk tarot card readers are not the only places you hear about the futures market. Financial pundits refer to the futures markets all the time, especially since recent hot commodities—like oil and corn—are directly tied to them. So are individual stocks.

Professionals use the futures market to make investment decisions about their stock holdings. That's because they know they can gather a ton of information about the current market environment just by watching and understanding the futures market.

There's a whole world of people out there that actually trade futures contracts and use them as hedges against their portfolio—just like you trade stocks. Quite frankly, there's more dollar trading volume in the S&P futures than in all the stocks in the NYSE combined. But trading futures can get pretty technical and risky. I don't like to take risks with my money, so we're not going there today.

Instead, we'll just focus on what you can learn by being a voyeur. Just watching and understanding the different movements in the futures market is enough to make you market savvy and think like a pro.

Shop at the Futures Market Today

The futures market is a centralized global marketplace for buyers and sellers to trade futures contracts. Think of it like your gym membership. You have one, right? When you signed up, you locked in at $75 a month for a year. That way it didn't matter that two months later the membership monthly fee jumped to $80. You were in a contract, so your price stayed at $75.

The futures market works the same way, except instead of paying for a gym you don't use, a jeweler might lock in the price of platinum for his upcoming engagement ring boom, especially if he thinks the price of platinum is going to increase. A futures contract will help him keep his costs down.

But commodities such as gold, oil, and platinum aren't the only futures trades. There are a few different futures markets, and they sometimes seem to get all garbled together.

There are financial futures, which are based on the stock markets, such as the S&P 500, the S&P 100, and the Russell 1000. The Chicago Mercantile Exchange web site has a complete list. There are commodity futures markets where things like corn, coffee, tobacco, and cattle are traded. Then there's the precious metals market, where you'll find gold, copper, nickel, and so on. The New York Mercantile Exchange site has a full list of the commodities trades. The rest of this chapter explains some of these markets in more detail.

Financial Futures

Futures contracts are available on individual stocks or the overall market. By trading financial futures, traders are essentially making a bet on the direction of a stock or particular segment of market. So someone who trades say, S&P 500 futures, is making a bet on the direction of the S&P 500. Basically, he's betting it'll either go up or down in the short term.

That's an important trade because it helps voyeurs like us get a feeling for the sentiment out there. That's exactly why the S&P 500 futures are one of the best directives of how our markets will do when they open at 9:30 A.M. in New York.

Here's why. Many big companies such as Intel (INTC), Microsoft, and General Motors (GM) trade overseas. If they had a good trading day in Europe, traders assume that same positive sentiment will carry over to the U.S. markets when they open. So they'll run out and buy S&P 500 futures contracts that presume the S&P 500 will be up, in the short term, in the U.S. markets. That overnight optimism generally means that our markets will open higher than they closed at 4 P.M. the night before.

Of course, this is no guarantee that the market is going to keep going higher. It's simply an indicator of how the day is going to start. So when you turn on the TV and hear that S&P 500 futures number, you'll have an idea of how U.S. stocks did overnight and what the traders think the market is going to look like when the market opens.

While you're half-listening and making your kids' lunch, you may also hear reports of a "fair value" comparison." This refers to the "fair value" of the S&P 500, which we won't get into here. What you need to know is that the relationship between the S&P 500 futures contract and the actual value, or *fair value,* of the S&P 500 is important. If the talking heads are saying that the S&P 500 futures are above the fair value, it is an indicator that folks are betting the overall index will go higher. If the S&P 500 futures are valued below fair value, traders think the index will go lower—just something to listen for as you rush your kids out the door in the morning.

The Future of Cattle and Corn

While watching the futures market in the commodities world won't necessarily help you predict the market for the day, it's just as important because many companies rely on commodities to run their business. The underlying trend in a commodity's price might be reflected in a stock's price.

Commodities are basically the stuff that goes into the production of other goods and services. Things like oil, corn, wheat, lumber, cattle, gold, and silver (platinum for girls like me) are all used in the production of the things we use so they're considered commodities. Changes in the price of these commodities can obviously affect the price of the goods that we purchase from certain companies.

Take a company such as Archer Daniels Midland (ADM). The company procures, stores, and processes agricultural commodities, and its core business is in oilseeds and corn processing. Any changes in the prices of those commodities have a huge impact on the stock.

If your company uses a commodity such as wheat, cotton, or lumber, pay attention to those particular markets. The numerous geopolitical factors that affect commodities pricing can also affect a stock.

Here's another good example: With all the recent talks about using ethanol (which comes from corn) as a substitute for gasoline, corn prices could continue to climb. But high corn prices won't bode well for a company like Kellogg (K) that has to buy loads of corn to make our favorite breakfast cereals that are expensive enough. An increase in corn prices could have a negative effect on Special K's stock. Hopefully, Kellogg is buying futures contracts on corn and locking in today's prices.

As another example, let's say there's a hurricane looming out in the Gulf of Mexico; the price of lumber may start to increase because people will be buying tons of plywood to protect their windows and will then need more if their homes get destroyed. If lumber goes up, your home builders feel the pain.

The Internet has additional information about the futures market, specifically:

- CME—Chicago Mercantile Exchange (www.cme.com)
- NYMEX—New York Mercantile Exchange (www.nymex .com)
- CBOT—Chicago Board of Trade (www.cbot.com)

No Option Is an Island

While you clearly shouldn't make buy/sell decisions strictly on what's happening in the options and futures markets, you can use them as a forecast to help you better understand the sentiment—or opinion—of investors and traders in your stocks. How your stock is faring will indirectly be reflected in both the options and futures markets, so use the options world as one more piece of data to support trading decisions.

Thanks to the transparency of information, the impact of expiration week doesn't move stocks nearly as much as it once did. Nevertheless, there is still a wealth of information you can derive from options trading.

Wrap-Up

Having choices is always a good thing. As a refresher:

- A *call* gives you the right to buy an asset at a certain price within a specific period of time. When you buy a call, you're betting the stock will go up and then you'll be able to buy shares at a cheaper price.
- A *put* gives you the right to sell an asset at a certain price within a specific period of time. Puts are bets that the stock price is going to fall. And when the shares do (presuming you bet accurately), you'll be able to sell your shares at a higher price.
- The *futures* market allows traders to place a bet on the future price of certain goods or indexes. They can lock in today's prices if they believe those prices will be higher going forward.

Watching the movement in the options and futures markets can give you a good sense of how people feel about your stock, especially during options expiration week. This is the third week of the month, when all options expire, or triplewitching, and when futures contracts expire as well. All that extra volume can be very telling. However, you don't want to place a bet on a stock based strictly on volume changes in the options market. Just use it as yet another metric that helps you make smart decisions.

The Chicago Board of Trade web site has a great strategy section that lets you simulate option trades so you can dabble in the options world without risking your paycheck (cboe.com/Strategies/DefaultEquity.aspx).

When you're ready to talk to your broker about buying options as insurance, you'll need to establish an options account. After that, buying and selling options should be relatively straightforward. If having a little insurance is going to help you stop tossing and turning in bed at night, then by all means, get educated so you can protect yourself.

Your ulcer—and your mattress—will thank you.

13

Bringing It All Together

Y ou're a market guru now. You understand the innards of stocks, bonds, mutual funds, and ETFs. You can comfortably walk through a set of financial statements, and you're armed with some great metrics to help you evaluate your stock picks. In addition, you understand how the Federal Reserve can play puppeteer with the economy. Excellent.

Now you need to put your newfound knowledge to work.

You need a plan. And you need a good one. Sometimes, investing in the markets is not unlike sitting down at the high-roller poker tables in Vegas. You can lose your shirt if you place a bet on the wrong stock or, even worse, leave your chips on the table for too long. That's the last thing we want to happen, so you need a sound strategy that will guide you when the market's up and when it's down, when there's talk of recession, or when it's a bull market. As I said at the beginning of the book, history has shown that the markets do go up over time. They just don't in a straight line. They zig and zag along the way. As I write this book in early 2008, many would argue that we were in a serious "zag," but a well-diversified portfolio can handle it.

While it's important to have a solid long-term plan, it's even more important to be flexible enough to make adjustments at times. This chapter describes strategies to consider while creating your ultimate portfolio.

1. Be Specific about Your Goals

You need goals. Sure, you have to save for retirement. I can spew tons of stats about how we're all financially unprepared, can't count on Social Security, and are destined to live in refrigerator boxes—but you know that already. For now, earmark part of your portfolio for retirement and be done. Then set fun goals, which make it easier to keep your eye on the prize.

For instance, in addition to saving for college for my three peanuts and my so-called golden years, I'm—no surprise here—saving for a Lamborghini. In addition, I'd love to buy a little pied-à-terre in Paris someday. Hey, these are my goals. They don't have to be yours.

So stop using vague phrases like "financial security" or "comfortable retirement," and start saving for specific goals such as your child's upcoming wedding or that RV you've been eyeing. Try saying things like:

> I want $1 million in the bank by the time I'm 60.

> I want an investment portfolio that will yield $2,000 a month to supplement my pension and Social Security.

Now that's something you can sink your teeth into. You can visualize those statements and that will help you stay on track.

In addition, I think everyone should have some money automatically transferred into an investment account on a monthly basis. Having good goals makes that transfer much more bearable.

Once you have your goals ironed out, start picking your investments to match your needs.

2. Spread the Risk Around

Diversification hedges your risk. You know that. Now you need to diversify your portfolio based on your goals:

- Longer-term goals allow for more time and, therefore, more risk. So think about the equity market here—stocks.

- If you need the money next year for your son's wedding, you better get that stash in cash quickly.
- Other midterm goals fall somewhere in between.

As you will recall, stocks are the riskiest investment you can make, bonds are less risky, and cash is as riskless as it comes (see Cash Is King for a Reason). So you need a decent percent of each. The old-school rule of thumb is:

- Stocks: 50 percent to 80 percent
- Bonds: 20 percent to 40 percent
- Cash: 10 percent to 25 percent

Cash Is King for a Reason

It sounds corny, but cash is an important part of the equation. The economy is a sketchy place these days. Between talks of recession, presidential elections, and the constant fear of terrorist attacks, nothing is a sure thing—including your job. You need some cash in the coffers.

Most financial planners suggest that you set aside three to six months' living expenses in a money market account or bank savings account. You're not looking to fund retirement with this money. It is not for your new car or your new condo in Miami. This money is there in case of that "God forbid" moment, as we Sicilians say.

So just put it aside and fuggedaboutit. I couldn't resist.

But you decide on those percentages based on your gut.

Yes, I'm talking about your stomach.

Is it queasy? Do you get nervous easily when it comes to money? Does it keep you up at night? You need your beauty rest, even if it means missing out on the next "Apple" (which, in early 2008, was up 1,500 percent over the last five years). I am so not looking to promote gray hair, so if you get uneasy easily, forget investing in IPOs, like we discussed in Chapter 11, or hot new biotech stocks. Instead, think big global companies such as McDonald's (MCD), Coke (KO), PepsiCo (PEP), and

Altria (MO). No matter what happens in the world and the economy, people need to eat, drink and, well, smoke. (Altria is the company makes Marlboros). That's why these stocks consistently do well over the years.

If you are a risk taker, then go ahead and dive into the riskier side of the market—just don't do it with your entire portfolio. Do it with a chunk of change you'd be willing to part with. Consider it your play money. It could be $500 or $5,000. It's just an amount you can live without because while you may be lucky enough to come across the next Apple, you may also end up investing in the next Priceline.com (PCLN), which is down 74 percent since its IPO in April 1999.

Personally, I'm not much of a gambler. I've never even played in Vegas or, closer to me, Atlantic City. I swear. I do realize that there are parts of the world and the economy that are up-and-coming and could potentially make me money. That's where I jump over to Knockoffville. A great way to spread the risk would be to buy just a few individual stocks and buffer them with mutual funds and ETFs as described in Chapter 4.

Use mutual funds and ETFs to get yourself exposure to sectors that you don't understand. For instance, I own the iShares MSCI Emerging Markets Index ETF because I have no interest or time to learn about the emerging economies of Argentina, Brazil, Chile, China, Colombia, Czech Republic, Egypt, Hungary, India, Indonesia, Israel, Jordan, Korea, Malaysia, Mexico, Morocco, Pakistan, Peru, Philippines, Poland, Russia, South Africa, Taiwan, Thailand, Turkey, and Venezuela. At the same time, I do believe there is a ton of growth potential in those places, so I want a piece of the pie. I just don't want to figure it out on my own. So I cheat with the ETF.

You can do the same with any other sector you don't feel like investigating.

Be honest with yourself. If you're a total techie, then you'll be stoked to follow the tech stocks. But if you have no interest in understanding what's going on in the financial arena, thanks to the subprime mess, consider a fund that covers it or the ETF, like the Financial Select SPDR (XLF), which holds the stocks of about 90 financial institutions including big banks such as Bank of America, Citigroup, and JPMorgan Chase.

3. Don't Marry Your Holdings

Marriage is tough enough. Don't put that kind of pressure on your investments as well. Don't get married to your portfolio holdings. The market is nutty these days. Just the utterance of words such as recession, terrorism, or lawsuits (especially out of the pharmaceutical stocks) can send the market into a tizzy.

You need to be flexible. Just because you spent hours analyzing a company with all the fabulous tips you learned in Chapters 5 through 10 and decided it was perfect for your portfolio at that point in time doesn't mean it will stay that way forever. So heed the following:

- Don't be optimistic at the top and pessimistic at the bottom. Optimism and bullishness are infectious, as are pessimism and bearishness. So keep focused.
- Don't follow the crowd. Don't assume that just because everyone else is buying something, you should, too. Market conditions change—they have to. So don't assume that what has been happening will continue forever. It can't, so be prepared for change.
- Don't ever buy on tips and rumors. Trust me, your cabbie, yoga instructor, and your sister's new stockbroker boyfriend all know nothing.
- Just because a stock is cheap doesn't mean it's worth buying. A stock that sells for peanuts is probably doing so because that's what the market thinks it's worth.

Similarly, don't bet on one industry. If you put all your money in financial stocks in 2007, you were probably in a state of complete panic by early 2008. So pick stocks across the different market sectors. Those sectors basically break the market down into 11 different market areas. Two are generally regarded as defensive, and the other nine are referred to as cyclical.

Defensive Sectors:	Cyclical Sectors:
Utilities	Transportation
Consumer staples	Technology
	Health care
	Financial
	Energy
	Consumer cyclical
	Communication
	Capital goods
	Basic materials

Owning stocks from the defensive sectors is key because companies in these areas typically don't experience much volatility when the market gets rocked. Basically, no matter what happens people still need to eat and use energy. So consider stocks like Procter & Gamble, PepsiCo, Coca-Cola, ExxonMobil (XOM), and BP (BP). Those are great choices for the defensive portion of your portfolio. And with the market turmoil of late 2007 and early 2008, these stocks were holding on.

There is a downside to defensive stocks, however. When the market is on fire, these stocks don't rise nearly as fast. They're slow and steady. Nothing wrong with that, though. Again, depending on your gut, you may want these stocks to make up the bulk of your portfolio.

Cyclical stocks cover the remaining market sectors and typically react to different market conditions. As a very simple example, if interest rates go up, the financial sector will suffer because people won't be borrowing money from the banks. (Your defensive plays will still be just fine, though.)

Understanding market sectors allows you to add protection to your stock portfolio. By investing in a number of different sectors, you can better hedge yourself from changes in the market.

Here's a very simple example. Let's say you put $11,000 in the financial sector in 2007. Thanks to the subprime fiasco, you lost about 25 percent of your investment, or $2,750, that year. If, instead you invested equally in the 11 market sectors listed above, even with the financials falling 25 percent, you would have lost only $250 or 2.3 percent of your investment, assuming the other sectors stayed neutral.

That wasn't an entirely realistic example, but you get the point: Diversify among the different sectors.

4. Do Your Homework

No one likes to do homework, but if you had any interest in getting into (and then out of) college, you had no choice. If want your stock portfolio to perform like a Harvard grad, you'd better do your stock homework as well.

That means understanding all the different nuances of the companies you choose to invest in. Just like you wouldn't just give your hard-earned money to some random financial adviser without scrutinizing his or her track record, you shouldn't give your money to a company's management team without doing the same due diligence.

While we all realize portfolio homework is a requirement, many of us just don't do it or, better yet, just don't know how to do it. So get out your assignment pads and write this down. I'm giving you an assignment. If you've gotten this far in the book, you're armed with all the knowledge and information you need to dissect stocks. Now you just need some direction on how to use all that newfound expertise.

Ideally, it would be great if you could do an hour of homework a week on each stock you own. I've divided your homework into two parts: the assignments that must be completed before you buy a stock and your weekly assignments once you own it.

Assignments before You Buy

Before you buy a stock, do these five things:

1. Go to the Securities and Exchange Commission's (SEC's) web site at www.sec.gov and pull up your company's

financials—the quarterly or annual reports—and dissect them. You know how to do that now. (For a refresher, go back to Chapters 5 through 7.)

Remember not to avoid the text. The company has a story, so read it. Understand exactly how the company makes its money. If it's in broadband, then you should be able to define "broadband" to anyone. If it makes children's clothes, then go buy some, let your kids wear them, and then send them through a wash cycle. Get personally involved with the product.

2. Understand the metrics, or ratios, that pertain to your company's business, as discussed in Chapter 10. This requires some number crunching, but you need to be aware that certain specific metrics are more relevant in certain industries. For instance, if you're looking at:

   ◆ *Cable companies.* Enterprise value (market cap plus debt) divided by the number of subscribers.
   ◆ *Hotels.* Average revenue per room.
   ◆ *Airlines.* Average revenue per seat.
   ◆ *Retailers and restaurants.* Same-store sales.
   ◆ *Tech stocks.* Gross margin per product sold.
   ◆ *Financial stocks.* Net interest margin (i.e., how much money was made on each dollar the financial institution had in assets).

   Once you know the key metric, compare it with the company's peers. The retailer with the best same-store sales, for example, is the one you want to own. So while all the numbers are important, some clearly hold more weight.

3. Listen to previous conference calls and read past analyst reports. The calls are generally available on your company's web site. You can either listen to them or read the transcripts.

   While research used to be hard to come by, these days there's a ton of good stuff available for free. The best place to start is with the broker you use to make trades. Odds are good there are research reports available to you, as a customer, on its web site. For instance, I have an account with Fidelity. I can go to its home page, click Research, Stocks, and then Browse Research Reports. A bunch of different reputable options come up, including reports from top firms such as Lehman Brothers, Standard & Poor's, and Thomson Financial. I enter the ticker symbol of the company I'm researching and a list of research reports pops up.

The same goes for a Charles Schwab (SCHW) account. All of its proprietary and third-party research is available to all clients free of charge.

In addition, check out Zacks.com. They write their own company reports, and they're easy to understand—and free! And you can also find analyst estimates on good financial site like my alma mater, TheStreet.com, in the earnings section.

4. Enter the company's name in a search engine and read all the latest news and stories that have been written on it.

5. Create mock portfolios on the Web. This is my favorite thing to do—and it's totally free. If you're thinking about buying a particular stock or stocks, create a pretend portfolio on sites such the Wall Street Journal Online (wsj.com) and Google Finance (finance.google.com/finance). You just plop in the tickers, name your portfolio and those sites will help you track the stock prices and gather the recent news on those holdings for you. This is a great way to help you decide if you want to buy the stock because you can actually watch it in action.

Once you complete those four assignments, you should be armed with enough information to decide if the stock's worth buying.

Assignments for Stocks You Own

Once you own a stock, you can't just forget about it. You need to spend time, at least once a week, on your holdings. The markets are far from stagnant, so the reasons you bought the stock could change on a dime.

Here are your weekly stock assignments:

1. Put your company's name in a search engine and read the latest news and stories that were written on it during that week.
2. Analyst reports get updated all the time. Read the latest versions to get an idea of how the analysts' thoughts are changing.
3. Figure out what's going on in the economy and how it affects your company. Will your stock get hurt because of the U.K. terrorist plot? If we have a harsh winter or interest rates ago up, is your stock affected? Determine how the overall economy plays into the future of your stock.
4. Decide it's still a keeper. At the end of your hour-long research session, you should have a definite answer on whether you need to buy more, hold, or sell.
5. Again, put your portfolios on the Web. Many sites will actually e-mail you any new news on your holdings so you instantly know what's going on.

If, after all that, you still can't come up with an answer on your stock, go do more homework.

So there are your assignments. Now get busy!

5. Don't Forget to Pay Uncle Sam

If you sell a stock or get a dividend distribution, expect to owe tax. Remember, Uncle Sam always gets a cut. And while the tax system can be as convoluted as a roomful of teenagers, I'll cut to the chase for you.

Capital Gains

If you sell a security—stock, bond, option, or fund—for more than you paid, you'll owe capital gains tax on the difference.

To calculate that difference, be sure to include your commission fees. Any commissions paid to purchase the shares are added to your basis, or purchase price. So if you bought

$100 worth of stock and paid a $5 commission to get those shares, your basis is $105.

Let's say you sold those shares for $125 13 months later. If you paid another $5 to make the trade, your proceeds are $120. That makes your total gain, or profit from the transaction, $15 ($120 – $105). This transaction should be reported on Schedule D, Capital Gains and Losses, and you'll owe capital gains tax on the profit.

The rate you owe will depend on how long you held the shares. If you held the shares for more than a year before you sold them, you'll qualify for the long-term capital gains rate, which is 15 percent (5 percent if your ordinary income tax bracket is 15 percent or lower).

Short-term capital gains are generated from assets held less than a year. Those gains are taxed at your ordinary income tax rate. So if you're in the 35 percent tax bracket and made $100 on a stock you held for four months, expect to owe $35 in capital gains tax. (See A Quick Word on the Wash Sale.)

The low long-term rates are expected to expire in 2008. While many folks in Congress are pushing for these rates to be permanent, keep that in mind for planning purposes.

You can apply your capital losses against your capital gains and potentially wipe out that tax bill. In addition, you can declare another $3,000 in losses (or $1,500 if you are married filing separately) on your tax return.

So let's say you have $15,000 in losses but only $10,000 in gains. You can offset that gain with $10,000 in losses. Of the $5,000 remaining losses, you can claim another $3,000 this year. The remaining $2,000 loss must be carried forward to next year. And you can carry forward those losses until they're used up.

Dividends

Dividends are always a nice perk from your stock or mutual fund holdings. Many of us opt to have those dividend distributions reinvested back into the asset. But remember, just because you don't get to play with that money doesn't mean you avoid the tax hit. If the mutual fund or stock that's distributing the dividend is in the toilet, that tax bill just adds insult to injury.

Most dividends qualify for a lower preferential 15 percent tax rate, though some are taxed at your ordinary rate, which could be as high as 35 percent. Your Form 1099 should tell you which rate you'll have to pay. And again, this lower 15 percent dividend rate is also scheduled to expire in 2008.

A Quick Word on the Wash Sale

The 30-day rule—the *wash sale rule*—can make or break your tax situation on a short-term trade, so you need to be familiar with it.

Basically, the wash sale rule states that if you sell a security at a loss, you can't deduct that loss on your tax return if you turned around and bought a "substantially identical" security 30 days before or after the sale. Shares of the same stock in the same company are considered substantially identical, according to the Internal Revenue Service (IRS). Preferred stock is not considered substantially identical to common stock, though.

Why? Because if you buy a stock, sell it at a loss, and then immediately buy it back, on paper, you're in the exact position you started. You're still holding the same stock that you started with. But by selling those original shares, you generated a juicy tax loss for yourself. The government doesn't think you should be able to deduct that loss on your tax return if you haven't really altered your position.

So let's say you sell your shares at a $1,000 loss, but you like the stock and really want it back in your portfolio. Just wait 30 days to buy the shares back if you want to take the loss. And then on day 31, you're in the clear, taxwise, and can buy away. At that point you can have both the stock and the tax loss.

Wrap-Up

So get going on your ultimate portfolio. Pick anywhere from 5 to 10 stocks to keep yourself diversified and stay on top of them.

I know you're busy, but now you know how to get a lot done in very little time. You understand what the pundits are saying now. So if the TV is on while you're making lunch for the kids in the morning, you'll know exactly what they're saying and will be able to ferret out the information you need to continue to make smart decisions.

Because that's really what it's all about at the end of the day: being smart, staying smart, and still getting your daughter to dance class on time.

And of course, one day buying that Lamborghini.

APPENDIX

Useful Resources

Stocks and Bonds

Yahoo! Finance

- finance.yahoo.com

Google Finance

- finance.google.com/finance

Percentage Calculator

- www.percent-change.com

Mutual Funds, ETFs, and Index Funds

FINRA Mutual Fund Expense Analyzer
apps.finra.org/Investor_Information/EA/1/MFETF.asp
xSEC

Mutual fund costs calculator

- www.sec.gov/investor/tools/mfcc/holding-period.htm

Financial Statements

Accounting Observer

- www.accountingobserver.com/blog

U.S. Earnings Calendar on Yahoo! Finance

- biz.yahoo.com/research/earncal/today.html

Earnings.com

- www.earnings.com/highlight.asp?client=cb

Federal Reserve

Economic Indicators

- www.economicindicators.gov

Fox Business Economy section

- www.foxbusiness.com/markets/economy.html

U.S. Census Bureau Economic Indicators

- www.census.gov/cgi-bin/briefroom/BriefRm

IPOs

IPO Home

- ipohome.com

24/7 Wall St.

- 247wallst.com

New York Times IPO Offerings Section

- dealbook.blogs.nytimes.com/category/ipoofferings

Options and Futures

Chicago Board Options Exchange (CBOE)

- www.cboe.com/LearnCenter/OptionsInstitute1.aspx

Chicago Mercantile Exchange (CME)

- www.cme.com/edu

Options Clearing Corp.

- www.theocc.com

New York Mercantile Exchange (NYMEX)

- www.nymex.com

Chicago Board of Trade (CBOT)

- www.cbot.com

About the Author

Tracy Byrnes is an on-air reporter for the FOX Business Network, where she reports daily from the floor of the New York Stock Exchange. She is a regular on Neil Cavuto's daily business show as well as *American's Nightly Scoreboard* with David Asman. She is also a regular panelist on *Cavuto on Business* on the FOX News Channel.

Byrnes is also an award-winning journalist specializing in tax and accounting issues. She has written columns for the *New York Post*, Wall Street Journal Online, and TheStreet.com. Her work has appeared in *Money* and *SmartMoney* magazines. She is the recipient of the Newswomen's Club of New York Internet Breaking Business News Award and the New York State Society of CPAs award for Online Excellence in Journalism.

Byrnes began her career at Ernst & Young LLP as a senior accountant. She has a B.A. in English and economics from Lehigh University and an M.B.A. in accounting from Rutgers University.

She is a pure-bred Jersey girl and still lives there with her three delicious kids.

Index

A&W All-American Food
     Restaurants, 8
AccountingObserver.com, 93
Accounts receivable, 75–76, 135
AFLAC (AFL), 30–31, 34
Alcoa (AA), 13
Altria (MO), 27, 29, 178
Amazon (AMZN), 120
American Express (AXP), 13
American International Group
     (AIG), 13
American Software (AMSWA),
     14
American Stock Exchange
     (Amex), 4, 5, 7, 15
Amgen (AMGN), 122
Analytical, 133
Anheuser-Busch (BUD), 34, 43
Annual report (10K), 64
     letter from the auditor, 67–68
     letter to the shareholders, 67
     Management's Discussion and
          Analysis (MD&A), 65,
          66–67
     10Q, 66
AOL (TWX), 81
Apple (AAPL), 4, 7, 12, 14, 120,
     121, 177
Archer Daniels Midland (ADM),
     170
Assets
     definition of, 70–71

intangible, 130
     net tangible, 130
AT&T (T), 13
Average selling price, 135
12b-1 fee (marketing fee), 50

Back-end load, 49–50
Baidu.com (BIDU), 121, 144
Balance sheet, 69–77
     accounts receivable, 75–76
     book value per share, 72
     debt-to-equity ratio, 73
     financial statements, footnotes
          to, 73–74
     inventory, 76–77
     leverage, 72–73
     purpose of, 70–72
Balanced funds, 46
Bank of America (BAC), 13
Barclay's Global Investors, 56
Basis points, 109–110
BCBS Bankcorp (BCBS), 93
Bear market, definition of, 105
Beer, nutritional value of, 48
Berkshire Hathaway, shareholder
     meetings, 9
Bernanke, Ben, 101, 103
BlackBerry, 12
Blockbuster (BBI), 93
Boeing (BA), 13
Bogle, John, 47
Bond funds, 46